PENGUIN BOOKS

THE PHILOSOPHY AND PSYCHOLOGY OF PERSONAL IDENTITY

Jonathan Glover was born in 1941 and educated at Tonbridge School and Corpus Christi College, Oxford. He is a Fellow and tutor in philosophy at New College, Oxford, and has written *Responsibility* (1970), *Causing Death and Saving Lives* (Penguin 1977) and *What Sort of People Should There Be?* (Penguin, 1983). He is married and has three children.

JONATHAN GLOVER

I

The Philosophy
and Psychology of Personal Identity

PENGUIN BOOKS

PENGUIN BOOKS

Published by the Penguin Group
Penguin Books Ltd, 27 Wrights Lane, London w8 5TZ, England
Viking Penguin, a division of Penguin Books USA Inc.
375 Hudson Street, New York, New York 10014, USA
Penguin Books Australia Ltd, Ringwood, Victoria, Australia
Penguin Books Canada Ltd, 2801 John Street, Markham, Ontario, Canada L3R 1B4
Penguin Books (NZ) Ltd, 182–190 Wairau Road, Auckland 10, New Zealand

Penguin Books Ltd, Registered Offices: Harmondsworth, Middlesex, England

First published by Allen Lane The Penguin Press 1988
Published in Pelican Books 1989
Reprinted in Penguin Books 1991
1 3 5 7 9 10 8 6 4 2

Printed in England by Clays Ltd, St Ives plc
Filmset in Bembo

Contents

═══

PART TWO: SELF-CREATION

To Vivette

PREFACE

====

DESPITE THE TITLE 'I', this book is not about me. It is about the personal perspective we each have on the world and, particularly, on ourselves. Throughout the book, points are made using the word 'I'. But they are general points, about the personal perspective of anyone. Very little can be learnt about my life from what is said, and I hope the frequent use of 'I' will not be seen as megalomania.

It has been necessary to draw on work in philosophy, psychology and neurology to develop the argument of this book. In at least two of these fields, I have had the sense of talking about things that others know much more about. But there is sometimes point in trying to give a broad picture of a central aspect of people, and such a project, unless carried out by a polymath, is likely to run into this difficulty. No doubt there are points in this book where those more knowledgeable would dissent. But something is lost if everyone sticks to their own special field and a larger picture is never attempted. I hope that the gains from trying to unite different perspectives compensate for the defects of the approach.

I am grateful to the British Academy for permission to use, in parts of Chapters Fourteen and Nineteen, material which was first used in my Henriette Hertz Lecture, published in the Academy's *Proceedings* in 1983.

I have been helped in discussion, and by the suggestion of helpful things to read, by more people than I can mention here. On the topics of the first half of the book, I have learnt more from Derek Parfit than from anyone else, first through discussion over many years, and then from his original and powerful book. Jonathan Miller has been very helpful about neurological issues, and has encouraged me to think that trying to link them with philosophy is worth doing. I have learnt also from Richard Keshen, both in discussions and through reading his book on partly overlapping issues. I am grateful to Richard Lindley for reading part of the book and making some acute comments on it.

I have been helped by students I have taught over many years. It is easy, getting deeper into an academic field, to take so much for granted that you end up talking in a way only others in the field understand. Or, even worse, you end up talking to yourself. But students challenge all this. They do not take for granted that if it is in the journals it must be worth talking about. In trying to explain, I have sometimes come to see that a thing is not worth talking about, and at other times I have become clearer why it is.

In this book, I have tried at times to write about some fairly abstract philosophical issues without losing people who are not already familiar with them. I will not always have succeeded, and will at times have irritated professionals by what they will see as simplifications. But I am sure the effort is worth making. If philosophers have anything to contribute to the world, we cannot always talk only to each other.

My wife has for many years discussed the human mind with me, and we have tried to link up her perspective as a neurochemist with my philosophical viewpoint. Parts of the book are the result of this. It was mentioned above that little can be learnt from it of my own life. There is an exception. Part of the book celebrates the way people shape each other by doing things together and by sharing their responses. My picture has itself been shaped by experience of this with Vivette

INTRODUCTION

═══

THIS BOOK IS ABOUT what it is
to be a person, to think of oneself as an 'I'. It is about the ways
people think of themselves, and how they use these ideas in shaping
their own distinctive characteristics. It is about how far we create
ourselves.

An individual person is unique and valuable. This value we place
on the individual finds expression in a cluster of ideas and attitudes.
People should be treated as ends in themselves, and never merely as
means. One person's loss is not necessarily justified by someone else's
gain. People have rights. And, linked to these ideas (psychologically
if not logically) is the pleasure we take in human variety, and a
preference for a society in which individuality flourishes.

These values are sometimes said to have emerged in Europe just
after the Middle Ages, and to be a distinctive feature of our descendant Western culture. Perhaps this is right, but our interest in the
individuality of ourselves and others is based on older and more
universal features of human experience. The idea of the unity and
uniqueness of each person is part of what is expressed by the religious belief in the soul. It is understood at some level by anyone
who thinks a friend is less replaceable than a car or a piece of furni-
ture.

The book falls into two halves. The first part is about what it is to
be a person. The second is about how we are able to create ourselves. It is also about the importance this ability has for us, and
the implications of this aspect of human nature for politics and
society.

Being a person
==

The two halves of this book each draw a picture. The first half, about being a person, is an attempt to show how work in science and philosophy converges to give a picture that is not the one natural to us. This part of the book draws particularly heavily on the work of others. Its aim, as far as is possible in such a controversial field, is to draw a map, giving an overall view of how work in different fields fits together.

Three central claims will be argued for. First, our natural belief that a person has an indivisible unity is mistaken. This will be supported by considering psychiatric and neurological syndromes in which, in various ways, people seem to divide. Some of these cases show how the unity of a person depends on neural links, which can be severed. Consciousness can be divided. And there is at least the theoretical possibility of a much greater degree of fragmentation. Understanding how to divide consciousness also suggests how we may be able to develop ways for people to share consciousness.

The second claim is that being a person requires self-consciousness. This depends on a certain unity. Except in pathological cases, we do have this unity to a high degree. The conditions for having it will be explored.

The third claim is that our natural beliefs about what our own unity consists in are mistaken. Strong challenges to these natural beliefs have come from recent work in philosophy. Our conceptions need to be defended against these challenges, or else revised.

This argument draws on evidence well known to psychiatrists, neurologists and psychologists. It draws on ideas and arguments from some of the historical philosophers, such as Hume, Kant and Wittgenstein. Some of their ideas are highly relevant to understanding issues that are still alive. But, because these ideas are often buried in off-putting philosophical systems, they are rarely taken up by those outside the world of professional philosophy. The picture also draws heavily on contemporary ideas in philosophy, notably on the remarkable contribution of Derek Parfit.

The 'map-drawing' aim of the first half of the book may need some defence, especially as it applies to the philosophical ideas. Such maps are not common in philosophy. This is for several reasons. It may seem that not enough is agreed for a map to be possible. Or it may seem that the most important philosophical ideas have often been developed in the context of the philosophical system of some major philosopher, and cannot be understood properly when wrenched out of that context. Or it may be said that the best current ideas have been developed using arguments of great subtlety, often making use of technical apparatus drawn from logic or semantics. Again there seems a problem for any map that aspires to be accessible.

The first difficulty, that there is less agreement in philosophy than in some other fields, is in part a real one. It can be the despair of students to find that the writers they read on a topic ignore each other, or else mention each other only to disagree. If nothing is ever argued to anyone else's satisfaction, there seems no hope of progress. And, without that, how can this endless meandering round the same questions possibly be justified?

If there were really as little agreement as the literature suggests, this scepticism would be unanswerable. But the impression is misleading. Philosophers do not make a reputation by stating their agreement with what others have said, so the points of disagreement are the ones that are highlighted. The 'map' approach becomes possible if, as I believe, there is often in philosophy a concealed area of agreement. (But in presenting things in this way, I hope that what I say will be judged on the arguments given, rather than on any appeal to the supposed authority of some philosophical consensus.)

The other objections to the 'map' approach have to do with the difficulty of extracting philosophical ideas from their context: either of some systematic theory, or of the technical apparatus used in their expression. We lose something if we take ideas and strip them of the subtle terminology designed for their precise expression. And, as with a poem, we may miss important aspects of a philosophical idea if we are ignorant of its context, historical and otherwise.

I am against most of this. Take one consequence of treating ideas as inextricable from systems. On this view, we can never compare what Hume, Kant and Hegel said about the self, because of uncertainty as to how far they were talking about the same questions. Taken to an extreme, this would mean that we could only compare their whole world-views with each other. This would make progress in philosophy very hard to assess. It would also make it very hard for progress to take place, as it would make it hard for successive philosophers to contribute to a debate on the same issue.

Another consequence is a disastrous one for philosophy. To learn about philosophy is partly to be introduced to the ideas and arguments created by philosophers in trying to answer philosophical questions. But it is also to learn to use rational methods in thinking about such questions for yourself. There is a kind of intimidation that makes thinking for yourself seem hopeless. It might take five years to get on top of the logical and semantic techniques used in current philosophy. It might take five years to get on top of Kant's philosophy. It might take between ten years and eternity to get on top of Hegel's philosophy. If these are all preconditions of worthwhile thinking about these questions, the project is probably not worth starting. A little casualness can be liberating.

I said that the two halves of the book each draw a picture. The pictures are in two different styles. The first picture, like much modern philosophy, is in a style that resembles abstract art. It argues in part by means of thought experiments: asking the reader to imagine various cases designed to sharpen the conflict between different theoretical views. Often the inner structure of a problem is best exposed by imaginary cases which are in some ways quite unrealistic. The lack of realism is unimportant for the purposes of the thought experiments. But, just as we would not try to use a Henry Moore or a Picasso for learning anatomy, so the thought experiments should be seen as theoretical tools, not as themselves studies in a realistic portrayal of people.

Self-creation

The second half of the book takes being a person for granted, and draws a picture of our active interest in what marks us off from other people. This second picture, of our shaping our own characteristics, is drawn in a different way. It is an attempt at the equivalent of representational rather than abstract art. It takes an aspect of our psychology, and tries to bring it into sharper focus. This is partly because of its intrinsic interest. It is also to suggest that this aspect of us is more important than is often thought, especially for our thinking about what society should be like. But this part of our psychology is not one where there is much agreed knowledge. There is little decisive evidence or argument to be drawn on. So the picture is inevitably more personal and subjective.

We each have a framework of beliefs about people. In the absence of dispute, we assume that our framework is the same as that of others. No doubt, there is usually a lot of overlap: we would be unlikely to understand each other as well as we do without it. But, when we discuss things, we often come to see that others do *not* accept things we had taken for granted that they would. Because of our assumption of agreement, we do not spell out the framework, and so never get clear about our differences. This is a way to make no progress in resolving them.

I shall be sketching out my picture of this aspect of people, together with some illustrative evidence which I hope will make it plausible. Of course, in a way, I hope the picture presented will be found convincing. But I take it for granted that most people will find this picture different from their own in various ways, and that they will often continue to prefer theirs to mine. If this picture provokes people to work out alternatives more explicitly, the resulting comparisons may make some progress possible.

Three claims will be made. The first is that the distinctiveness of a particular person is not something just given, but is something we partly create in the course of our lives. My distinctiveness is affected by choices I make. Decisions about relationships, about what work to do, or where to live, may be influenced by how I see my life so far, and by my ideas of what sort of person I want to be. And these decisions, in turn, lead us to grow in one direction rather than another.

The possibility of shaping ourselves needs to be defended against two related forms of scepticism. One version says we are entirely the product of the various social pressures on us during our lives, and that these pressures leave no room for any effective choice to be one sort of person rather than another. The other version is more plausible, but not more comforting. Perhaps social pressures leave us some area of free play, but our use of it is in turn determined by other factors. This more complicated determinist picture poses an obvious threat to the possibility of free choice. The second claim of this part of the book is that the scientific picture of human beings does not exclude our partly creating ourselves in the light of our own values.

The third claim is that our partial creation of ourselves is *central* to what we are like. Although usually hardly noticed, it is one of the things we most value in life. And because of this, our thinking about what makes a good society should take more account of it.

Certain beliefs and values occupy an unchangingly large place in our picture of things. So they are background, and we notice them as little as we do the sky. Coming to see the centrality of self-creation leads to more understanding of other things. It helps to explain why, even if we give up the traditional explanations of the unity of a person, that unity does not disappear, and why the boundaries between people remain important. It has some implications for the kind of society we should hope for. It may shed some light on relationships. Finally, it may help us understand the stubborn tribal loyalties whose daily toll fills the news bulletins.

PART ONE

WHAT
IS A
PERSON?

CHAPTER ONE

MULTIPLE
PERSONALITY

ONE WAY OF THINKING about what it is to be a person is to look at cases where there is doubt about where one person ends and another perhaps begins. Such anomalous cases are found in both psychiatry and neurology. Here we will start with some of the psychiatric cases.

Some people seem to be possessed at different times by different personalities. These 'personalities' can vary in voice, mannerisms and handwriting. They can call themselves by different names. One may be left-handed when others are not. In an American case, one personality spoke with an English accent and knew Arabic, while another knew Serbo-Croat and spoke English with a Yugoslav accent.[1] And, notably, each of them has a very different general style. One thirty-nine-year-old woman had six of these personalities, including Mary, 'a nun who preached sacrifice', and Deborah, a 'screaming lady who recounted the many traumatic incidences of sexual molestation and perverse rituals at the hands of the patient's aunt and grandmother'.[2]

Normally the 'host' personality reports an inability to remember stretches of life when another personality has been in control. This reported amnesia is not always mutual: sometimes one personality clearly has access to the doings of another. In the case of Sally Beauchamp, studied by Morton Prince, one of the personalities, Chris, played practical jokes on Miss Beauchamp, making her tell absurd lies, and delighted in her resulting embarrassment.[3]

[1] D. Keyes: *The Minds of Billy Milligan*, New York, 1981.
[2] William F. Clary, Kenneth J. Burstin and John S. Carpenter: Multiple Personality and Borderline Personality Disorder, *Psychiatric Clinics of North America, Symposium on Multiple Personality*, 1984.
[3] Morton Prince: *The Dissociation of a Personality, the Hunt for the Real Miss Beauchamp*, London, 1905.

In the early years of the century, a number of cases of multiple personality were reported, but there was a decline until about 1970, possibly because cases of this type were more often classified as schizophrenia. The 'voices' that some schizophrenics hear inside their heads generate a similar sense of part of 'me' being taken over by someone else. But multiple personality is once again a more common diagnosis. One recent estimate puts the number of cases current in the United States at about a thousand.[4]

Multiple personality is so strange that many have been reluctant to accept its existence. But it is not a completely isolated syndrome. There is the similarity with some features of schizophrenia. It also has something in common with sleepwalking, which people often forget having done. And people under hypnosis sometimes seem to divide: in 'automatic writing', a hand writes about one thing while the rest of the person is occupied with something quite different. And there have been cases reported of 'fugues', where someone walks out of one life and lives for a time as a quite different person, with apparent amnesia for the earlier life.

There is some evidence of physiological differences between the different personalities. When someone is shown a repeatedly flashing light, the resulting electrical activity in the brain appears as a wave on the electroencephalogram. Each person has a distinctive wave pattern. Some research on people with multiple personality suggests that the different personalities have different wave patterns. The evidence is conflicting. In some studies, the differences found were greater than in controls asked to think themselves into different imaginary personalities, but in one study the control produced differences that were as large.[5]

There is evidence that multiple personality appears particularly often in people who report having been abused as children, either physically or psychologically. The patient whose personalities included the screaming Deborah is in this way fairly typical, although the form the abuse is said to have taken is bizarre. Among the 'perverse rituals' forced on her by her aunt, Deborah reported 'drinking the ashes of dead mice that were roasted in an oven and mixed in

[4] Bennett G. Braun, in *Psychiatric Clinics of North America. Symposium on Multiple Personality*, 1984.

[5] Frank W. Putnam: The Psychophysiologic Investigation of Multiple Personality Disorder, a Review, *Psychiatric Clinics of North America, Symposium on Multiple Personality*, 1984.

a potion', as well as 'attempts to force her to eat faeces and drink menstrual blood'.

The link with childhood trauma suggests how multiple personality might arise. It may be very hard to form a single picture of yourself that includes both normal relationships (friendships with other children, and with adults outside the family) and your role as victim of these assaults. One way of coping with this would be to compartmentalize your life, behaving as different people in the different contexts.

There are other cases where aspects of someone's life that are hard to integrate with each other are treated in a similar way. There are people whose job includes torture and other atrocities, but who return in the evening to their role of being good-natured husbands and fathers. How can the family man putting his children to bed live with the screams of his victims of the afternoon?

One plausible account is in terms of what Robert Jay Lifton, in a study of doctors who worked in Auschwitz, has called 'doubling'. This is the development of a psychological barrier so that the person at home and the person at work feel nothing to do with each other. Lifton says:

Use of the term *doubling*, rather than mere splitting, calls attention to the creation of two relatively autonomous selves: the prior 'ordinary self', which for doctors includes important elements of the healer, and the 'Auschwitz self', which includes all of the psychological manoeuvres that help one avoid a conscious sense of oneself as a killer. The existence of an overall Auschwitz self more or less integrated all of these mechanisms into a functioning whole, and permitted one to adapt oneself to that bizarre environment. The prior self enabled one to retain a sense of decency and loving connection.[6]

It is almost as though one life is lived by two people at different times. If this is a plausible account of concentration camp doctors, it may fit others with a double life, such as bigamists and spies.

It is *almost* like two people sharing a life. The lack of identification found in such cases is not multiple personality. When the Nazi doctor goes home, this does not bring on literal amnesia about his work. In the case of multiple personality, the suggestion is that child abuse presents a similar problem of integration, but that the child's

[6] Robert Jay Lifton: Medicalized Killing in Auschwitz, *Psychiatry*, 1982.

strategy for dealing with it is more drastic, leading to barriers of amnesia between the compartments.

Problems of interpretation
==

There is no doubt about the existence of psychiatric patients who present the psychiatrist with the kind of history that fits the diagnosis of multiple personality. But it is unclear how this evidence should be interpreted.

The most sceptical interpretation is that the patients are malingering. There have been cases which at least raise that suspicion. An English politician in business difficulties appeared to have drowned in Florida, but was later found living in Australia as a different person. This might appear to be a case of a fugue, but the misleading evidence of drowning, as well as other features of the case, left open the possibility of a less charitable interpretation. And, in an American murder case, where a man was accused of being the 'Hillside Strangler', the defence argued that a different personality had committed the crimes. Sceptics have argued that the suspect had access to his psychiatric records, and so could shape his responses accordingly.

The desire to escape from problems, or to avoid criminal conviction, could provide a strong motive for pretending to multiple personality. And less crude motives could have the same effect. Self-dramatization, and the ability to make oneself exceptionally interesting to a psychiatrist, could motivate deception.

A determined sceptic could interpret any alleged case of multiple personality as fraud. The motive of self-dramatization may be present, and the psychiatrist may be naive. But, to support the view that all 'multiple personality' is malingering, a moderately impressive amount of evidence would have to be explained away. The differences between the personalities often seem to go well beyond the normal capacity for acting. And the link with being abused as a child is suggestive. It is conceivable that child abuse could lead to adults feigning disorders they do not have. But it seems more likely to lead to a genuine psychiatric syndrome.

If we are inclined to accept that a fair number of the cases are genuine, we still have alternative interpretations. The person is, in some sense, divided. We are dealing with two or more relatively independent functional systems controlling behaviour at different times. But this could be interpreted as a strong kind of division, with two or more people, each independent and conscious, inhabiting one body. Or the division could be something weaker: perhaps more like the 'doubling' of the torturer, bigamist or spy, but with the addition of amnesia. There are several possible weaker kinds of division. A secondary personality might function unconsciously, or it might be partly under the control of another personality. Or, as in the case of Miss Beauchamp, another personality might have access to its experiences, either at the time or through memory.

The strong version of division conflicts with our normal view of people. And, as often happens when claims are made about strikingly deviant phenomena, the attitudes people adopt form a radical-conservative spectrum. Radicals say that we must adjust our picture of what people can be like in the light of these cases. Conservatives say the strong version of division is so bizarre that it is implausible that it really occurs.

The debate is parallel to those about ghosts, miracles, telepathy and other claims that do not fit the conventional picture of the world. One problem with all these debates is the vagueness of the standards of plausibility. Most of us agree that we need more evidence in support of a cure by a miracle than in support of one by surgery. But it is hard to see just how much extra evidence it is rational to require. Clearly the existence of alternative explanations affects our view of such claims. Where malingering is ruled out, the conservative strategy for resisting strong claims about multiple personality is to favour explanations which minimize either the independence or the consciousness of the secondary personalities.

What kinds of division exist must ultimately be decided on empirical grounds, by examining cases in detail. But, because assessment of the evidence is influenced by standards of plausibility, there are theoretical questions too. Multiple personality clashes with our normal beliefs in three ways. The thought that what someone does is a product of sub-systems (independent centres of control within the person) conflicts with our ordinary ideas about the unity of a person and about our awareness of our own mind. Such division as part of a motivated strategy for coping with problems seems to require implausibly strong powers of voluntary fragmentation. And the idea of such a sub-system being an independent centre of consciousness is a further departure.

But there are reasons for thinking that these barriers have already been breached. These reasons, if accepted, may reduce the apparent implausibility of relatively strong versions of multiple personality.

Unconscious sub-systems

==

Consider first the question of sub-systems. There is evidence for the occurrence of subliminal perception: information flashed on a screen too quickly for conscious awareness seems to enter part of a person's mind. There is evidence that it can influence subsequent perception, what people say, and even the contents of later dreams.[7]

There is also the striking phenomenon of 'blind sight'. People with some kinds of brain damage become blind in one half of the visual field. But, although they have no experience of seeing anything in the 'blind' half, they sometimes seem capable of absorbing information from that half. If they are asked to point to a spot of light on a screen on their blind side, they say they cannot see it and that they are only guessing its position. But they are able to point to it correctly far more often than by chance. When asked to grasp an object in their blind half, they move their arms, hands and fingers in ways that show some knowledge of the object's position and orientation. There is also some evidence that they can take in words presented in their blind half, again without any conscious awareness of seeing them.[8]

This unconscious processing of information is a pervasive feature of our mental life. Most of us are familiar with forgetting someone's name, turning aside from trying to remember it, and the name later coming to us. It seems likely that this is the result of some unconscious process of memory search rather than just coincidence. And there are cases of people being puzzled by an intellectual problem which suddenly solves itself by an unexpected intuition, either in a dream or at some other time when the question has been put aside.

Some famous examples are of mathematical discoveries by Henri

---

[7] N. F. Dixon: *Subliminal Perception, The Nature of a Controversy*, London, 1971.
[8] L. Weiskrantz, Elizabeth K. Warrington, M. D. Sanders and J. Marshall: Visual Capacity in the Hemianopic Field Following a Restricted Occipital Ablation, *Brain*, 1974.

Poincaré. (Some readers will share my relief that Poincaré's description can be followed without knowing what the mathematical terms
refer to.) He had been thinking about a problem for two weeks
without much success, when he went on a geological excursion.

Having reached Coutances, we entered an omnibus to go some place or other.
At the moment when I put my foot on the step, the idea came to me, without
anything in my former thoughts seeming to have paved the way for it, that the
transformations I had used to define the Fuchsian functions were identical with
those of non-Euclidean geometry. I did not verify the idea; I should not have
had time, as, upon taking my seat in the omnibus, I went on with a conversation
already commenced, but I felt a perfect certainty. On my return to Caen, for
conscience' sake, I verified the result at my leisure.[9]

There are other cases. The way Kekulé discovered the ring structure
of benzene was by having a dream of snakes intertwined in the
appropriate pattern. And Loewi dreamed how to do the experiment
which showed that the transmission of nerve impulses between
neurons involves chemical change.

As with remembering the forgotten name, it seems likely that
some unconscious sub-system has been at work on the problem in
the intervening period. We have grown accustomed to the possible
truth of the Freudian idea that we are unconscious of some of our
motives and emotions. But this evidence about thinking and about
information retrieval suggests that a lot of mental activity with no
particular emotional charge also takes place unconsciously.

Consciousness is sometimes represented as a process by which the
brain monitors its own states. We are used to the idea that some
things the brain does are not monitored in this way: we are not
conscious of the way it controls heartbeat or breathing. It seems that
some intellectual activities also can be hived off to sub-systems not
consciously monitored.

Self-deception
==

It may still seem unlikely that we can deliberately hive off sections of
our life to this kind of oblivion. But this is suggested by the account
of multiple personality as a defensive response to child abuse. Is it

[9] Henri Poincaré: *Mathematical Creation*, quoted in Jacques Hadamard: *The Psychology of
Invention in the Mathematical Field*, Princeton, 1945.

possible deliberately to shield some aspects of ourselves from our own consciousness? There are paradoxes here which have to be avoided.

Self-deception is very familiar. We tell ourselves we are good athletes, explaining away races we lose by our lack of preparation or by the state of the track. We are very intelligent, and the IQ tests which underrate us have obvious defects. We stand a reasonable chance of winning the lottery, but we are very unlikely to be among those killed on the roads . . .

Despite its familiarity, self-deception is problematic. Taking the idea of deception literally suggests that we adopt a conscious strategy of concealing certain things from ourselves. But how can I be at the same time deceiver and deceived? If I know enough to adopt the strategy, surely I know too much to be taken in by it? Self-deception presents the disturbing appearance of being both widespread and impossible.

One way of eliminating the paradoxical element of self-deception would be to treat the self-deceiver as really being two people, one consciously deceiving the other. The model might be the strong interpretation of multiple personality, with the behaviour of the deceiver towards the deceived resembling the practical jokes played on Miss Beauchamp by Chris. But this seems far too dramatic an account. It is hard to think that everyone who is motivated to overestimate their own attractiveness or their ability has such deeply divided consciousness. Multiple personality is not *that* common.

Apart from this drastic approach, there are two ways of avoiding paradox, which may correspond to two kinds of self-deception. On one version, the deception is incomplete. On the other, it is unconsciously motivated. Perhaps lumping these two weaker phenomena together as self-deception has led to an illusory belief in a stronger (paradoxical) case, where deception is both consciously carried out and complete.

The incomplete version is where we are motivated not to spell out or investigate things we suspect. We have an uncomfortable suspicion that a lump may be cancer, which makes us reluctant to see the doctor. Suspecting we are overspending, we do not keep a running total of our bank balance. This is self-deception, but we are not fully deceived. We are aware both of our suspicions and of our strategy of not investigating them. We do successfully shield ourselves from something: we may still get a shock when we learn the full position from the doctor or from the bank statement. But the paradox is removed because what is known to us as deceiver (grounds for suspicion) is not lost to us as deceived, and what we keep from ourselves as deceived (the full story) is not known to us as deceiver.

Other versions, where the strategy is unconsciously motivated and carried out, can bring about complete deception. Suppose the company I work for dismisses me, in a move that takes me completely by surprise. I had thought I had been doing well there. But, when I look back, I can see previously overlooked signs of their loss of confidence in me. Someone else was put in charge of some difficult negotiations; I was not asked to various meetings; and so on. If it had been anyone else, I would have been in no doubt what it all meant, but when it happened to me, I was able to explain away each bit of evidence without being aware of any need to do so.

The way we assess evidence usually depends on our standards of plausibility, which are rarely spelled out in any detail. This leaves room for manoeuvre which can be exploited by unconscious preferences for the more comfortable belief. At the time there need be no awareness of the bias: we are not consciously rejecting evidence, but unconsciously discounting it. There is no paradox because there is no conscious awareness of the real import of the discounted evidence. That is confined to an unconscious sub-system. The mind is divided, but, unlike multiple personality, the sub-system at work is unconscious.[10]

It is this second type of self-deception, if its existence is accepted, that provides a model for one feature of multiple personality. If a sub-system can adopt a strategy of keeping something from consciousness, it becomes (a bit) less extraordinary to see separation of larger sections of someone's life from the central consciousness as part of their strategy for responding to problems.

Are conscious sub-systems possible?

If we are prepared to accept that there can be sub-systems functioning independently of the central consciousness, and that they can have strategies of their own, we may still find the claims about multiple personality hard to accept. Perhaps the most extraordinary feature is that the sub-systems seem to be conscious. Are there any other

[10] Such sub-systems are well discussed in D. F. Pears: *Motivated Irrationality*, Oxford, 1984.

phenomena which may make two centres of consciousness in one brain seem less outlandish?

There are two kinds of case that can be cited. One, the topic of the next chapter, involves the cutting of the neural links between the two hemispheres of the brain. The other kind of case has been found in hypnosis.

A blind student was hypnotized and it was suggested to him that he would become deaf. He then became unresponsive even to very loud sounds close to him, and also to any questions he was asked. The hypnotist wanted to test whether 'some part' of the student was aware of the sounds. He quietly said to the student that there may be unconscious intellectual processes and that, although the student was hypnotically deaf, 'perhaps there is some part of you that is hearing my voice and processing the information'. He added, 'If there is, I should like the index finger of your right hand to rise as a sign that this is the case.' The finger rose. The student asked for his hearing to be restored, saying, 'I felt my finger rise in a way that was not a spontaneous twitch, so you must have done something to make it rise, and I want to know what you did.' His hearing was restored. Asked what he remembered, he said he remembered going deaf, and thinking about a statistical problem to avoid boredom, until he noticed his finger lift. Ernest Hilgard, who reports this episode, uses the metaphor of the 'hidden observer' to describe intellectual processes detached in this way from the person's stream of consciousness.[11] In the case of the hypnotized student, the 'hidden observer' later gave informed answers to questions about what had happened during the period of hypnotic deafness. But the student, questioned after that, seemed not to know what had been said.

A determined sceptic might suggest the possibility of the student playing a joke on the hypnotist. But such explaining away would have to be repeated for a number of other cases of apparent division of consciousness reported to have been hypnotically induced.[12]

If we accept the existence of the hidden observer in these cases, we have something closer to multiple personality than any of the other kinds of fragmentation mentioned so far. Taken together, subliminal perception, blindsight, unconscious problem-solving and self-deception should weaken the grip on us of the traditional picture

[11] Ernest Hilgard: *Divided Consciousness: Multiple Controls in Human Thought and Action*, New York, 1977, chapter 9.
[12] References to other studies are given in Hilgard: op. cit.

of the unified mind, all accessible to consciousness. And perhaps the most natural interpretation of the hidden observer takes us further, so that we come to accept different centres of *consciousness* within a single person. Though even this falls short of the elaborate version of divided consciousness claimed for multiple personality.

A sceptic, who accepted the reports of the hidden observer, might say that the hidden observer is a sub-system which monitors events and answers questions about them all unconsciously.

We can see these episodes as instances of unconscious sub-systems, or as cases of divided consciousness. Part of the difficulty in deciding between these alternatives is the general obscurity of the criteria of consciousness. On what basis do I believe you are conscious? How far down the evolutionary scale does consciousness extend? Would a robot that functioned just like a human, but whose 'nervous system' was made of silicon, be conscious?

It seems that, very roughly, we ascribe conscious states to beings sufficiently like ourselves in what we take to be the relevant ways. You behave like me, and have a functionally similar nervous system, made of the same sort of stuff, so I have no serious doubt that you have conscious experiences. The higher animals are sufficiently similar in these ways to qualify. But, as we go down the evolutionary scale, complexity of behaviour and of nervous system tails off, so that few of us would be very confident about the experiences of a slug. And robots present a problem because we are not sure whether similarity of function is all that is required, or whether what we are made of makes a difference.

In these ways, our criteria are vague or disputed. (There are further questions. Do we know our criteria are the right ones? Is it possible that they sometimes give the wrong answer, including some beings who really do not have experiences, and excluding some that do? Or is there no fact of the matter, no such thing as 'really' being conscious, independent of our criteria?)

I have no answer to these difficult questions. But a sub-system within the human brain seems more likely to be conscious to the extent that the complexity of its functioning approaches that of a normal human being. Apart possibly from multiple personality, by far the best cases are those of people whose two hemispheres have been separated. These well documented cases make multiple personality seem less isolated. And they are themselves a remarkable demonstration of personal fragmentation.

CHAPTER TWO

===

SPLIT
BRAINS

The first observation I make at this point is that there is a great difference between the mind and the body, inasmuch as the body is by its very nature always divisible, while the mind is utterly indivisible.

RENÉ DESCARTES: *Meditations on First Philosophy*, 1641.

The totality of our mental life, as complex as it may be, always forms a real unity. This is the well-known fact of the *unity of consciousness* which is generally regarded as one of the most important tenets of psychology.

The fact of the unity of consciousness, as we have explained it, must then be considered to be indubitably certain.

FRANZ BRENTANO: *Psychology from an Empirical Standpoint*, 1874.

The 'patient' who speaks to you is not the 'patient' who is perceiving – they are, in fact, separate.

NORMAN GESCHWIND: *Disconnexion Syndromes in Animals and Man*, 1965.

Oᴜʀ ɪᴅᴇᴀ ᴏꜰ the unity of consciousness is a hazy one. Different kinds of experience can co-exist within a united consciousness. I see, hear and smell wine being poured into a glass, and this differs from the way three different people see it. But it is hard to say anything illuminating about this difference. It can, rather unhelpfully, be described as one of 'availability'. My visual, auditory and olfactory experiences of the wine being poured are 'directly' available to me at the same time. I can only know about your experiences of it by inference, either from where you are and the direction of your gaze, or from your behaviour and what you say. Cases where the hemispheres of the brain are separated force us to think more critically about this difference of availability.

The two hemispheres of the human brain play many complementary roles. Take the sense of smell: each nostril sends signals to the hemisphere on the same side of the body. With the sense of touch, matters are reversed. If the right side of the body is touched below the neck, signals are sent to the left hemisphere. The right hemisphere receives signals from the left side of the body. When we see, the hemispheres deal with different halves of our visual field, though each hemisphere uses information from both eyes. The right half of the visual field is scanned by the left half of the retina in both eyes. The two left halves send signals to the left hemisphere. The right hemisphere gets information by a parallel route from the left half of the visual field. The division of labour is not always so symmetrical: speech is normally controlled by the left (dominant) hemisphere, while the right (minor) hemisphere is mute. (In this discussion, I shall refer to the dominant hemisphere as the left one, and refer to the minor hemisphere as the right one. This ignores complications about left-handed people.)

There are minor links between the hemispheres through the brain stem, but the major direct link between them is the corpus callosum. It and some other linking neural pathways together form the cerebral commissures. Cutting these commissures reduces the communication between the hemispheres to the very minimal level that can take place through the brain stem. The commissures have sometimes been cut deliberately. This surgical operation (commissurotomy) has been found to be a successful treatment for severe epilepsy.

For a long time this treatment for epilepsy seemed unproblematic. There seemed to be no striking changes in the people whose hemispheres were separated. Scientists even wondered whether the corpus callosum had any function. But R. W. Sperry and others carried out some remarkable experiments on people treated in this way, which changed the picture.[1]

What happens if the content of the two halves of the visual field is different, so that the two halves of the brain are sent different visual information? We cannot study this by presenting the two eyes with different material, because each eye connects with both hemispheres. The way round this is to ask the person to gaze at a particular point, and to give different signals on the two sides of this central point of

[1] R. W. Sperry: Brain Bisection and Mechanisms of Consciousness, in J. C. Eccles (ed.): *Brain and Conscious Experience*, Heidelberg, 1966.

fixation. In the first studies, the signals were flashed on a screen long enough to be seen, but too briefly to allow the eye movements that would let them enter the other half of the visual field. Later studies used contact lenses fitted with a device which excludes input from one half of the field, however the eye is moved.

The results of these studies have suggested to Sperry and to others that commissurotomy leads to 'two separate conscious entities or minds running in parallel in the same cranium, each with its own sensations, perceptions, cognitive processes, learning experiences, memories, and so on'. What is the basis for saying this? It is that information fed into one hemisphere seems unavailable to the other.

The person may be asked to pick out from a set of things hidden behind the screen the one whose name is flashed up. Suppose 'key ring' is shown on the screen, with 'key' to the left of the central point (and so being sent to the right hemisphere) and 'ring' in the right half of the field (and so being sent to the left hemisphere). If asked what word appeared on the screen, the person replies 'ring'. (Speech is controlled by the left hemisphere.) The right hand (also controlled by the left hemisphere) will reject a key and pick up a ring. But the left hand (controlled by the right hemisphere) will reject a ring and pick up a key.

A natural interpretation is that each hand is controlled by a different centre of consciousness, obeying different instructions, each unaware of the aims of the other. This is supported by cases of apparent conflict between the hemispheres.

In one reported case a pipe was put out of sight in the person's left hand, and he was asked to write, with that hand, what it was.[2] The hand laboriously writes 'PI'. The writing suddenly speeds up and the word is turned into 'PENCIL'. Then 'ENCIL' is crossed out and the hand draws a picture of a pipe. It is plausible that the right hemisphere started the word; then the left hemisphere guessed what it was supposed to be, and interfered to complete it; and then the right hemisphere took over again to correct the mistake.

Sperry describes another case of conflict, in which 'the left hand, after just helping to tie the belt of the patient's robe, might go ahead

[2] Jerre Levy, Information Processing and Higher Psychological Functions in the Disconnected Hemispheres of Human Commissurotomy Patients, unpublished doctoral dissertation, California Institute of Technology, 1969, quoted in Thomas Nagel: Brain Bisection and Unity of Consciousness, in Mortal Questions, Cambridge, 1979, page 153.

on its own to untie the completed knot, whereupon the right hand would have to supervene again to retie it'. The left hand also sometimes 'tried to push the wife away aggressively at the same time that the hemisphere of the right hand was trying to get her to come and help her with something'.[3] Similar conflict took place in a woman described by Kurt Goldstein, whose left hand tried to strangle her.

All this seems to support the view, popular with those who have carried out the studies, that commissurotomy results in two minds within a single skull. But there has also been resistance to this interpretation. This is not just because of reluctance to accept anything so sharply in conflict with what we are used to. The main obstacle to the 'two minds' account is the apparent normality of the people when they are outside the experimental set-up. It is worth remembering that it used to be doubted whether, apart from reducing epilepsy, commissurotomy had any effects at all. It is puzzling how two independent minds controlling a single body can together lead what looks like a single coherent life.

Disconnections and confabulation
==

These cases are not the only instances of apparent disunity brought on by brain lesions. Neurologists have reported cases of brain injury in which the higher organizational levels of perception, thought, language or action are disrupted.

Some of the most striking cases are those traditionally classified as agnosia, or 'disorders of recognition'. Norman Geschwind and Edith Kaplan described a patient who was unable to name an object held in the left hand, although he could draw it afterwards and could pick it out of a group of things, using either sight or touch.[4] He could name objects held in the right hand without trouble. His ability to select the correct object from a group suggests the problem was not a perceptual one. It appears to have been a 'disconnection syndrome', caused by the severing of neural links. The part of the right hemi-

---

[3] Sperry: loc. cit.
[4] Norman Geschwind and Edith Kaplan: A Human Cerebral Disconnection Syndrome, *Neurology*, 1962.

sphere receiving tactile input from the left side of the body was cut off from the speech area of the left hemisphere.

There is a problem with this explanation. The patient did give (wildly misleading) descriptions of things in his left hand: when holding a coin, he said it was a cigarette lighter. If the speech area is totally disconnected from the relevant sensory area, it is puzzling that he could give any description of it at all. But, Geschwind suggested,

The fact that 'the patient' (i.e. the speech area) gives a description does not mean that we are getting an actual description of the perceptions going on in another disconnected part of the brain. We must again remember that we are dealing with more than one 'patient' here. The 'patient' who speaks to you is not the 'patient' who is perceiving – they are, in fact, separate.[5]

But if the questions are answered by the part of the person with no tactile awareness of the left side of the body, it is then puzzling why any answers, even wrong ones, are given. This seems to be a case of 'confabulation', something found by neurologists in people suffering damage that causes gaps in their sensory information. This happens, for instance, with scotoma, where damage to part of the retina means that part of the visual field cannot be seen. These patients often extrapolate from the information about the rest of the field to fill in the gap. This is like the process which causes normal people to be unaware of the blind spot in their visual field.

There are several things that could be going on in confabulation. One possibility is that the person is quite unconscious, both of the blank and of the process of filling it in, as we normally are of the visual blind spot. At the other extreme, the person might be fully aware of the blank, but, because of embarrassment, might deny it and knowingly invent the details. Or confabulation could be somewhere on the continuum between these cases. There could be a vague sense of something missing, and a way of filling in the gap that is somewhere between a conscious invention and a plausible guess. In many cases of disconnection syndromes there is some confabulation. The difficulty of being sure which kind it is adds to the problems of seeing exactly what psychological changes have taken place.

[5] Ibid. See also Norman Geschwind: Disconnexion Syndromes in Animals and Man, *Brain*, 1965.

Rival interpretations of the split brain studies

There is disagreement about the experimental studies of the commissurotomy patients. There are five main rival interpretations:

1. Their consciousness is not divided, because the minor hemisphere, which does not control speech, is not conscious.

2. Their consciousness is divided only during the experimental studies, and is unified in everyday life.

3. Their consciousness is divided at all times. (This does not rule out the possibility of later recovery through new links between the hemispheres being developed.)

4. Their consciousness is divided, but only in a way that brings out the previously unrecognized fact that we all have a divided consciousness all the time.

5. None of these explanations fits all the facts, and so we have to give up our normal assumption that we can make any sharp distinction between one stream of consciousness and two.

The questions that need to be considered are:

(a) Is it possible for consciousness to divide?

(b) Do the split brain patients have divided consciousness during the experiments?

(c) Is their consciousness divided at other times?

(d) Do normal people have a divided consciousness?

(e) Can we keep a sharp distinction between one stream of consciousness and two?

Can consciousness divide?

There is an argument against the possibility of consciousness dividing, based on our inability to imagine this from the inside. Descartes held that 'we cannot conceive of half a mind', and argued that 'when I consider the mind, or myself in so far as I am merely a thinking thing, I am unable to distinguish any parts within myself: I understand myself to be something quite single and complete'.[6]

This argument was expressed by Erwin Schrödinger (writing before the split brain studies). He said that 'we know that a sub-mind is an atrocious monstrosity, just as is a plural-mind – neither having any counterpart in anybody's experience, neither being in any way imaginable'.[7] He refers to 'the empirical fact that consciousness is never experienced in the plural, only in the singular', and goes on to defend it as something stronger than an empirical fact: 'We are not able even to imagine a plurality of consciousnesses in one mind. We can pronounce these words all right, but they are not the description of any thinkable experience.'[8]

This line of thought has some intuitive force. If you try to imagine your own stream of consciousness dividing, you always imagine the period after the split from the point of view of *one* of the resulting streams. I can only imagine the world from one perspective at a time.

But, as Kant pointed out,[9] this unity of perspective does not prove the indivisibility of the mind. A film is seen from the single perspective of the camera. From this it does not follow that the audience watching it must be one single person. Nor would it follow from the film's other unity: that sound is synchronized with vision. (Kant referred to 'the illusion which leads us to regard the unity in the synthesis of thoughts as a perceived unity in the subject of these thoughts'.)[10]

The limits of what I can imagine from the inside are not the limits of what is possible. I cannot imagine the division of my mind from both the resulting perspectives together. But equally I cannot imagine being both you and me simultaneously. Despite this, you and I still have separate minds. There are incompatible perspectives on the world. It is not a problem that they cannot be simultaneously adopted: that is what incompatibility is.

Schrödinger sees that his argument tells as much against different people having separate minds as against sub-minds. He accepts this implication: 'Mind is by its very nature a *singulare tantum*. I should

---

[6] René Descartes, Sixth Meditation, in *The Philosophical Writings of Descartes*, translated by John Cottingham, Robert Stoothoff and Dugald Murdoch, Cambridge, 1984, volume 2, page 59.

[7] Erwin Schrödinger: *Mind and Matter*, Cambridge, 1967, page 145.

[8] Ibid., pages 140–141.

[9] Immanuel Kant: Transcendental Dialectic, Second Paralogism, in *Critique of Pure Reason*, translated by Norman Kemp Smith, London, 1929.

[10] Ibid., A 402.

say: the overall number of minds is just one.'[11] But this conclusion can be treated as casting doubt on the premises. This way of ruling out divided consciousness requires us to believe that there is only one mind in the universe. Rather than accept this, we should allow that a stream of consciousness can divide.

Is the patients' consciousness divided during the experiments?

The case for saying that, during the experiments, the split brain patients have two independent streams of consciousness is an obvious one. Each hemisphere seems unable to draw on information given to the other, and they embark on independent courses of action, sometimes even coming into conflict with each other.

The alternative view is that, in the experiments, only the left hemisphere is conscious. (On a weaker version of the view, only the left hemisphere is *known* to be conscious.) This account sees the right hemisphere as carrying out complex tasks, but doing so unconsciously, perhaps as a computer might. Sir John Eccles and Sir Karl Popper see this account as one that adds to the plausibility of their dualist view of the mind, according to which a non-physical 'conscious self' interacts with the left hemisphere alone. As Eccles puts it, 'The outstanding discovery in the investigation of these subjects is the uniqueness and exclusiveness of the dominant hemisphere in respect of conscious experience.'[12]

Eccles uses a major argument and a minor one to support the rejection of any minor hemisphere consciousness. The minor argument appeals to a thought experiment. He says:

A gedanken experiment reveals the fundamental differences between the responses of the dominant and minor hemispheres. After commissurotomy with left hemisphere dominance the conscious subject has voluntary control of the right forearm and hand, but not of the left, yet the left forearm and hand can carry out skilled and apparently purposive movements. In our gedanken experiment the left hand inadvertently grabs a gun, fires it and kills a man. Is this murder or manslaughter and by whom? If not, why not? But no such questions

[11] Schrödinger: op. cit., page 145.
[12] Karl R. Popper and John C. Eccles: *The Self and its Brain, An Argument for Interactionism*, London, 1977, pages 311 and 315.

can be asked if the right hand does the shooting and killing. The fundamental difference between the dominant and minor hemispheres stands revealed on legal grounds.[13]

Perhaps we should call in the lawyers more often. When do philosophers or scientists solve these problems at such speed?

The major argument gives a more serious reason. It cites the inability of the minor hemisphere to speak. Eccles uses this point to support only the weaker claim, that we do not know that there are conscious experiences associated with the minor hemisphere. But how likely is it that consciousness is absent?

Inability to speak is not loss of all linguistic ability. We have seen that the minor hemisphere can respond to verbal instructions, and that it can retain some ability to write. But even if all language ability were wiped out, the conclusion would not follow. It is dubious that language is essential evidence for consciousness. Why ignore all the non-verbal evidence of consciousness that can be found in people who cannot speak or write, but who in other respects lead a normal life?

Some people have their left hemisphere surgically removed in adult life. If the linguistic limitations of the right hemisphere really showed 'the exclusiveness of the dominant hemisphere in respect of conscious experience', such people would be unconscious robots, and having the operation would be subjectively the same as death. But to those who know them they seem recognizably to be people with an inner life of their own.

It seems that, when the left hemisphere has been removed, the right hemisphere can be associated with consciousness. It is hardly likely that the presence in the same skull of a disconnected left hemisphere changes this. And so it is reasonable to see the disconnected right hemisphere of the split brain patient as a centre of consciousness. If this is right, the experiments do demonstrate divided consciousness.

Is their consciousness divided at other times?

If we accept that these patients have divided consciousness during the experimental studies, there is an obvious case for thinking they do so at other times. It is hard to accept that consciousness divides and

[13] Ibid., page 329.

unites when people enter and leave the experimental set-up. It is simpler to suppose that the operation just divides consciousness, rather than supposing that it somehow combines with the experimental conditions to cause a series of temporary divisions.

But there are two kinds of evidence that appear to tell against persisting division of consciousness. First, the patients report a more complete form of experience than one would expect. And, second, their behaviour in everyday life shows an extraordinary degree of integration.

The patients report a wider range of experience than we might expect to be available to the left hemisphere. They say their visual field is not impaired, and they report some sensations on the left side of their bodies.

But these claims are not fatal to the 'divided consciousness' view. There is evidence that the division of consciousness displayed in the experiments is accompanied by confabulation. Michael Gazzaniga and Joseph LeDoux report that the patient P.S. would carry out left and right hemisphere tasks simultaneously, but repeatedly produced a confabulation to explain the movements used in carrying out the right hemisphere task. The right hemisphere, shown a picture of snow, would pick up a card with a shovel on it. The left hemisphere, shown a picture of a chicken claw, would pick up a card with a chicken on it. Asked what he saw, P.S. said, 'I saw a claw and I picked the chicken, and you have to clean out the chicken shed with a shovel.'[14] Given this tendency to confabulate, it is possible to interpret the apparently unimpaired visual field as a larger scale version of the gap-filling response to retinal damage.

The other problem for the 'divided consciousness' view is the striking integration of their normal behaviour. After the operation, the patients live apparently normal lives. They can do things needing co-ordination of both sides of the body: doing up their shoes, or pouring from a jug into a glass held in the other hand. Without the experiments, no division of consciousness would have been suspected. And, as Thomas Nagel says, 'The people who *know* these patients find it natural to relate to them as single individuals.'[15] (However,

---

[14] Michael S. Gazzaniga and Joseph E. LeDoux: *The Integrated Mind*, New York, 1978, page 148.
[15] Thomas Nagel: Brain Bisection and Unity of Consciousness, in *Mortal Questions*, Cambridge, 1979, page 159.

these responses to them are not decisive. It is not clear what behaviour would be appropriate towards persons we thought had
divided consciousness. How would we speak to only one of them?
What would happen about eye contact?)

Does the high degree of left–right integration in normal life rule
out divided consciousness? Nagel says, 'There is little doubt that
information from the two sides of their brains can be pooled to yield
integrated behavioural control.' The question is whether there is
pooled information at one centre of conscious control, or whether
what goes on is more like the performance of two acrobats who
have had much practice at mutual co-ordination.

The 'acrobat' interpretation is given some support by the use to
which past habits could be put. Consider the advantages, for co-
ordination between two control centres, of their having previously
been one. Suppose the union between England and Scotland were
abolished, and the two countries became totally independent of each
other. The train services now provided between London and
Edinburgh by British Rail would be run jointly by English Rail and
Scottish Rail. The history of unified control would make co-
ordination easy: the old timetable would be continued. But it would
be a mistake to look at the smoothly running service and infer that
there must still be a single centre of control.

The 'acrobat' interpretation is also supported by the way some
of the integrated behaviour can be explained by cross-cueing:
the use by one hemisphere of the perceived response of the other.
For instance, when the right hemisphere is asked questions to
which only the left hemisphere knows the answer, its responses are
correct no more often than by chance. But soon scores improve
when a second guess is allowed. This is because the left hemisphere
is aware of the wrong answer being given, and starts to give a
frown or nod of the head, which in turn is detected by the
right hemisphere. This kind of mutual feedback helps to explain
how a high degree of integration could exist despite divided
consciousness.

This view of cross-cueing has been challenged. Charles E. Marks
has suggested that we could regard cross-cueing as a strategy serving
to unify consciousness.[16] If the exchange of information between the
hemispheres through the corpus callosum can unify consciousness,

[16] Charles E. Marks: *Commissurotomy, Consciousness, and Unity of Mind*, Montgomery, 1980.

why should not consciousness equally be unified when information is exchanged by a more roundabout route?

One problem with this suggestion is that the more roundabout route is very like that used when information is transferred between two different people. In reply to this, Marks says that, unlike what goes on between two people, cross-cueing seems unconscious: the 'two' minds seem unaware of each other's existence. But, even if it is unconscious, it is still an 'external' inference from behaviour. People normally do not learn about their own minds in that way. No inference from behaviour is required for me to report on the contents of the left half of my own visual field. It is plausible that a single centre of consciousness requires the direct pooling of information provided by neural links. That is a more convincing basis than is provided by inferences from behaviour, which are the way separate minds learn about each other.

The evidence about the split brain patients does not *easily* fit any of the natural interpretations available. The view that they have divided consciousness in normal life requires explaining away both their own accounts of their experience and their capacity for integrated action. I have tried to argue that accounts which explain away this countervailing evidence are more plausible than views which retain the unity of consciousness. If this is right, the experimental set-up does not cause division of consciousness. It is more reasonable to accept that the patients have divided consciousness the whole time.

Do we all have permanently divided consciousness?

The most dramatic conclusion that has been drawn is that, even without commissurotomy, there are two independent centres of consciousness in the normal person.

Roland Puccetti, who has argued for this view, appeals to cases where a complete hemisphere is removed.[17] Whichever hemisphere is left, there remains a person. He says that, if people were unitary, these operations should leave only half a person. He says that he can only explain the completeness of the remaining person by supposing

[17] Roland Puccetti: Brain Bisection and Personal Identity, *British Journal of the Philosophy of Science*, 1973.

that, before the operation, there was not a unitary person. 'He or she was a compound of two persons who functioned in concert by transcommissural exchange. What has survived is one of two very similar persons . . .' He goes on to mention 'the untalkative right brain-based person I have been verbosely overruling most of our lives'.

This conjures up a horrendous picture of the life of the minor hemisphere person. It must be terrible to be trapped, unable to protest, inside the same skull with someone else who does all the talking and takes all the main decisions.

Fortunately, there is little reason to believe this account. The fact that so much of a person survives the removal of either hemisphere shows that the two-hemisphere brain has the safety margin of a lot of redundancy. It need not be taken as showing that there were two people in the normal brain before the operation. In the British Rail network, there are alternative routes between London and Edinburgh, so the service would survive the destruction of one of the routes. But we do not have to conclude that British Rail now must be two independent systems, one of which has managed to hog all the publicity to the detriment of the other, neglected one.

It is plausible to interpret split brain patients as having divided consciousness because of the ways in which they are not like normal people. In the rest of us, the corpus callosum is intact, and we would have no difficulty in Sperry's experiments. Admittedly, commissurotomy is not the only way of causing divided consciousness. We have seen that a 'hidden observer' can be produced by hypnosis. But, where the neural links are intact, and hypnosis is not present, there is no reason to postulate more than one centre of consciousness. Integrated behaviour based on functioning neural links gives no basis for such a view. We can accept divided consciousness in split brain patients without having to see it in everyone.

Ways of counting minds

How should we count minds in these difficult cases? A possible way is suggested by the analogous problem of whether a cultural or linguistic group within a larger country should have separate nationhood. Should Scotland, Quebec, or the Basque region of Spain become fully autonomous nations? One answer appeals to self-determination. If French-speaking and English-speaking Canadians want to be separate from each other, they should be. On this analogy, if the mental lives of the two parts of the brain both include a general attitude that they are separate from each other, then they are separate minds.

Self-determination is not the easy solution it seems. Asking the two hemispheres about their attitudes may not yield a clear answer. Neither hemisphere may have thought of the possibility of being two people. Or, if they have, the parallel with the nationhood case may go further: they may not agree on how they see their relationship.

An alternative version of the self-determination policy is, instead of asking the views of the hemispheres, to devise some behavioural test of their attitudes. An ingenious attempt at this has been made by D.M. and Valerie MacKay.[18] J.W. was an epilepsy patient whose corpus callosum had been severed. Each hemisphere was trained to play a game of guessing which number the other could see. The hemisphere which knew the number responded to guesses by pointing to one of three answers on a card: 'OK', 'go up', or 'go down'. The game was played for tokens, which were won by correct guesses. Each token would buy one piece of information about which way to go when a guess was wrong.

The experimenters tried to create a conflict of interest between the hemispheres. They claim that they did not succeed in creating conflict of policy. They see this as (admittedly negative) evidence for the view that the person is only partly divided: split at the level of transfer of information, but not at the level of decision-making.

The possible conflict of interest was introduced by asking the hemisphere that knew the answer if it would like to be paid more for information. It indicated it wanted three tokens. This stopped the game by bankrupting the other hemisphere. At this point it was suggested that the (right) hemisphere which knew the answers might settle for less. The left hand (controlled by the right hemisphere) pointed to 'two tokens'. At the same time, J.W.'s mouth (controlled by the left hemisphere) said, 'Sure, make it two tokens'. This

[18] D.M. and Valerie MacKay: Explicit Dialogue Between Left and Right Half-Systems of Split Brains, *Nature*, 1982.

unanimity is taken as (inconclusive) support for the existence of a
unified decision-taking system.

However, two unambiguously separate people could have reached
the same unanimity. Often in children's games such compromises
are reached when the game continuing is more fun than the immediate bankrupting of your opponent. So this study does not give the
self-determination approach the decisive test it needs.

I have argued that the 'two minds' view gives the best account of
the kinds of integration and lack of integration that are found. But
this is compatible with accepting that 'minds' may have fuzzy edges,
so that counting them may be a rather blurred affair. Several factors
contribute to the fuzziness. Behaviour can be integrated to varying
degrees, and this may vary at different times. Perhaps, as the MacKays
suggest, decision-taking can be integrated without there being the
'direct availability' that comprises the unity of experience. Or, con-
versely, perhaps there could be unity of experience and yet conflicts
between rival decision-taking systems. In such cases there might be
no single 'right' way of counting how many minds are present.

Partly, what matters is how far one or more than one functional
system is present. There does not have to be an unambiguous answer
to this. In a network of several computers linked together to different
degrees, is the functional unit the computer or the network? I have
tried to give reasons for the view that split brain patients, unlike the
rest of us, are better seen as two functional systems than as one.

But, as we can see from cross-cueing and from pairs of acrobats,
unified functioning' as shown in behaviour is not all that matters.
There also has to be some kind of unity of consciousness and control.
And some of the most striking conclusions to be drawn from these
studies are not about how many minds are present. They are that
there can be fuzziness in the answer to this, and that unity of consciousness depends on what neural links are severed or joined.

CHAPTER THREE

===

THE FRAGMENTATION
OF CONSCIOUSNESS

The sense impression I have of green exists only because of me, I am its bearer. It seems absurd to us that a pain, a mood, a wish should rove about the world without a bearer, independently. An experience is impossible without an experient. The inner world presupposes the person whose inner world it is.

GOTTLOB FREGE: *The Thought: A Logical Inquiry.*

THE UNITY OF CONSCIOUSNESS depends on neural links. This unity is reduced or destroyed by those links being cut. It is roughly correct that splitting a brain in two splits a mind in two. How far can the process of fragmentation go? The unity of consciousness at any one time involves such things as my simultaneously seeing and hearing a car go past. Could this unity be fragmented by disconnecting neural links between the visual and auditory systems?

C. S. Sherrington once speculated that there might be 'quasi-independent sub-brains based on the several modalities of sense', and asked, 'How far is the mind a collection of quasi-independent perceptual minds integrated psychically in large measure by temporal concurrence of experience?'[1] Since Sherrington's time, the split brain studies have suggested that more is needed for psychological unity than just experiences taking place at the same time. There must also be the right neural links. But the idea of partly independent sub-brains suggests the possibility that brain injuries might lead to separate visual, auditory and tactile minds.

Here I am not concerned with what will in fact turn out to be empirically possible, but rather to construct a thought experiment. Perhaps the different sensory systems share too many neural pathways

[1] C. S. Sherrington: *Man on His Nature*, London, 1940, chapter 9.

for their separation to be possible. For the purposes of this discussion, suppose (perhaps improbably) that no such difficulties exist. Suppose we can sever the links underlying the unity of sensory experience, while keeping the senses functioning. (There are some models of the brain used for teaching which can be dismantled and re-assembled like a three-dimensional jigsaw puzzle. Think of the real brain as if it were like this.)

If we could keep sensory systems functioning when isolated, this would perhaps create non-communicating visual, auditory and tactile minds. Consider, along the same lines, detaching from the rest of the brain the neural network responsible for awareness of pain. Would stimulating this network cause pain? Has a neurophysiologist a serious reason not to stimulate it? Or is it absurd to suppose that there could be such an isolated experience of pain?

The case against isolated experiences is expressed in Frege's objection to a pain being able to 'rove about the world without a bearer'. A pain system detached from the rest of the brain would presumably lack any ability to conceptualize. It could have no thoughts, so any awareness it had would not reach the level of the thought 'I am in pain.' But is this any reason at all to deny that it experiences pain?

Some philosophers have been sceptical about whether at that sub-intellectual level there is any possibility of experience. Kant argued that 'It must be possible for the "I think" to accompany all my representations; for otherwise something would be represented in me which could not be thought at all, and that is equivalent to saying that the representation would be impossible, or at least would be nothing to me.'[2]

There are two components of this scepticism. One version doubts the possibility of 'raw' experience, not interpreted by any set of concepts. Since Kant, many philosophers have emphasized the close links between having experiences and our ability to classify and interpret them. Kant is often understood as claiming that the ability to use certain concepts to interpret experience is a condition of having experiences at all. But this may be too strong. In the passage quoted, he allows an alternative possibility: a 'representation' which could not be interpreted 'would be impossible, or at least would be nothing to me'.

[2] Immanuel Kant: *Critique of Pure Reason*, translated by Norman Kemp Smith, London, 1929, B 132.

Kant was perhaps wise to leave open these alternatives. One sounds like something trivially true: certainly uninterpretable experience *means* nothing to me, and perhaps this is the same as it being nothing to me. The other alternative is that a being without the intellectual equipment to interpret experiences cannot have them. This would need a strong argument or some good evidence to make it convincing. Without such backing, it seems dogmatic to assert that any creature with a nervous system must either have these powers of interpretation or else be completely unconscious.

The other component of the Kantian scepticism links experiences to self-consciousness. The suggestion is that any experience must belong to some mind that is aware of itself having an experience.

Objections to 'impersonal' experiences

The isolated pain system cannot *think* of experiences as being painful. But let us suppose that this is not a decisive objection to the existence of experiences caused by stimulating the system. The other possible objection is that total inability to think or classify rules out self-consciousness. These experiences are impersonal, in that they do not belong to any self-conscious mind. There is no one who can think, 'This experience is mine.' And it is doubtful whether there can be experiences which no one is aware of having. How can an experience be painful if no one is finding it so?

This problem is central to the discussion of Descartes' celebrated proof of his own existence. Trying to find securely based knowledge of the world, Descartes considered the possibility that all his present beliefs might be false.

But immediately I noticed that while I was trying thus to think everything false, it was necessary that I, who was thinking this, was something. And observing that this truth *I am thinking, therefore I exist* was so firm and sure that all the most extravagant suppositions of the sceptics were incapable of shaking it, I decided that I could accept it without scruple as the first principle of the philosophy I was seeking.[3]

[3] René Descartes: *Discourse on Method*, part 4, in *The Philosophical Writings of Descartes*, translated by John Cottingham, Robert Stoothoff and Dugald Murdoch, Cambridge, 1984, volume 2, page 127.

One common criticism of Descartes' argument is that he was wrong to deduce from the existence of a thought the existence of a thinker who has it. Lichtenberg said, 'We know only the existence of our sensations, presentations, and thoughts. We should say, *It thinks*, just as we say, *It lightens*. It is going too far to say *cogito*, if we translate *cogito* by *I think*.' [4]

The success of this criticism of Descartes depends on whether there could be the kind of impersonal experience suggested by the phrase 'It thinks.' There are two kinds of difficulty for this idea. One is whether it is even intelligible. The other is whether it leaves any distinction between an impersonal experience that is part of my mental history and one that takes place in the mental life of someone else.

The first problem with 'It thinks' is that this formulation is supposed to allow the possibility that, although an experience exists, no one is having it. But it is far from clear what this could mean. To speak of experiences which no one has may be to wrench words out of the context that makes them intelligible. It may be like talking of a grin without a face, or of a conversation that happened without anyone taking part in it. There is a danger in talking of 'experiences' as if they were things, separable from their owners in the way hats are. Once an experience stops being a state of a person (me feeling hot, or you thinking about your holiday) and becomes free-floating, we may lose grip on what it is meant to be.

When Lichtenberg said that Descartes should only have claimed that 'It thinks', he did not mean that this impersonal thought *could* not have belonged to Descartes, but only that Descartes should not have assumed that it did. So these impersonal experiences are meant to be things that can turn out to be part of someone's mental history. The problem about such impersonal experiences concerns the difference between their belonging to one person and belonging to someone else.

Kant considered an argument designed to show that a thinking mind cannot be composed of separable parts:

For suppose it be the composite that thinks: then every part of it would be a part of the thought, and only all of them taken together would contain the whole thought. But this cannot consistently be maintained. For representations (for instance, the single words of a verse) distributed among different beings, never

[4] Quoted in Ernst Mach: *The Analysis of Sensations*, New York. 1959, page 29.

make up a whole thought (a verse), and it is therefore impossible that a thought should inhere in what is essentially composite.[5]

This may not be a good argument against thought taking place in something divisible (such as the brain). Kant himself rejected it. But it does bring out a problem for the view that thoughts are impersonal. If every person in a group is thinking a word, the fact that the words will combine to make a sentence does not mean that there has occurred the thought which the sentence expresses. Even if the words are thought in the right order, it makes a difference whether they form part of a single stream of consciousness or whether they appear in different ones.

Bernard Williams has put the problem well, saying that we need to 'relativize' thoughts.[6] We need to mark the difference between what is part of this stream of consciousness and what is part of another. For this, we need to go beyond 'It is thought' to 'It is thought here.' But, as Williams points out, 'here' is totally figurative, and it is hard to see what sort of 'location' can be given except by reference to the person who has the thought: the kind of location normally indicated by 'I'. This objection suggests that 'impersonal' thoughts when fully spelt out turn out to be personal ones.

If we do not elaborate the idea of impersonal experience in some such way, there is a problem of how we can even understand what it means for someone else to have an experience. I learn that 'There is a pain' is true when (as we should normally say) I have a pain. And because this is what the sentence means to me, I may interpret it in that way even when the pain is in another body. As Saul Kripke (expounding a version of Wittgenstein's views) puts it, 'In sum, any attempt to imagine a direct connection between a sensation and a physical object without mentioning a "self" or "mind" leads me simply to imagine that *I* have a sensation located elsewhere.'[7]

In this way, the Lichtenberg approach, thinking of experiences only impersonally, is in danger of sliding into the belief that *my* experiences are the only ones there are. This is sometimes seen as a consequence of doubt about whether the evidence we have is good enough for us to *know* that other people are conscious. But what

[5] Kant: *Critique of Pure Reason*, Second Paralogism.
[6] Bernard Williams: *Descartes, The Project of Pure Enquiry*, Harmondsworth, 1978, pages 95–101.
[7] Saul Kripke: *Wittgenstein on Rules and Private Language*, Oxford, 1982, page 133.

threatens us here goes deeper than that. The problem is whether we even *understand* what that assertion (or its denial) means.

This sceptical conclusion is one most of us wish to avoid. But, if we think of experiences in purely impersonal terms, we can only avoid the conclusion by finding some way of 'locating' them. And when they are located, perhaps they are now personal.

Sub-personal experience
==

The problems that arise for Lichtenberg's purely impersonal conception of experience are serious. We cannot understand the idea of free-floating experiences, which, as Frege put it, 'rove about the world'. ('The window was not open wide enough for a burglar. But perhaps a few loose experiences managed to get in.') And, if we try to talk about experiences in a way that is not tied to the context of a particular stream of consciousness, it is hard to retain the distinction between one mind and another.

Where does all this leave the neurophysiologist wondering whether it is wrong to stimulate the isolated pain system? Are the objections to Lichtenberg enough to show that only a person can have experiences? The conditions for being a person may not be very clear, but it is hardly plausible that the isolated pain system satisfies them.

The objections to Lichtenberg leave open the possibility of experiences being had by something less than a person. (Unless 'person' is *defined* as anything that has experiences.) The objections rule out free-floating experiences, detached from any particular stream of consciousness we can identify. We normally identify a particular stream of consciousness by the person it belongs to, and usually identify the person in turn by physical characteristics. In the case of the isolated pain system, we are not considering free-floating experiences. They are ones we can locate in the stream of consciousness which is caused by stimulating this particular neural network. Objections to free-floating experiences do not necessarily rule out sub-personal ones.

I am inclined to think it would be wrong for the neurophysiologist unnecessarily to stimulate the pain system. This is on the grounds that it might be conscious. The moral objection rests partly on the belief that pain is an evil even if not had by a person. But it also rests on accepting that the philosophical arguments do not rule out the possibility that the pain system is conscious, or even show that this is unlikely.

But from this it does not follow that such consciousness is likely either. At least at present, we have very little idea of what degree of neural complexity, or what kinds of neural integration, are required for consciousness. So we should keep an open mind about the extent to which fragmented consciousness is possible.

Perhaps consciousness survives extreme fragmentation. But, if so, the resulting state is mainly interesting for what it lacks. We are persons through having the kinds of integration that enable us to transcend such states.

CHAPTER FOUR

INTEGRATION

Suppose the mind to be reduc'd even below the life of an oyster. Suppose it to have only one perception, as of thirst or hunger. Consider it in that situation. Do you conceive any thing but merely that perception? Have you any notion of *self* or *substance*? If not, the addition of other perceptions can never give you that notion.

DAVID HUME: *A Treatise of Human Nature.*

THE SPLIT BRAIN STUDIES raise the problem of how minds are to be marked off from each other. We have to decide whether it is more reasonable to say that the split brain patient has one mind, two minds, or perhaps something between one and two. The relevant evidence for functional unity is partly how integrated the patient's behaviour is. But we have seen that, because of cross-cueing and the possibility of a well-coordinated team performance, integration of behaviour does not guarantee unity of mind. Unity of consciousness is needed as well.

Two kinds of unity are relevant. There is the unity of consciousness at one time: I see the moor and the sky, hear the birds, and feel myself walking, all as part of a single integrated experience. And there is the unity of consciousness across time: as I walk across the moor, my experiences change, but they flow smoothly into each other as part of a single story.

Unity of consciousness at one time is not just a matter of different experiences occurring simultaneously. Suppose there is a procession, where half the people taking part are deaf and the other half blind. (It is some kind of celebration in an early Buñuel film.) There will be many visual experiences and at the same time many auditory ones.

But none of this generates the unified experience of both seeing and hearing the procession.

Some philosophers have been very puzzled about how the unity of consciousness is to be accounted for. David Hume started by thinking of experiences in impersonal terms: we are aware only of the experiences themselves, not of any 'I' which has them. But he came to think that the question of what integrates a stream of such experiences over time is perhaps an insuperable problem for that view: 'But all my hopes vanish when I come to explain the principles, that unite our successive perceptions in our thought or consciousness. I cannot discover any theory, which gives me satisfaction on this head.' [1]

Hume's difficulty, like the one about the unity of consciousness at one time, comes partly from assuming that the explanation must be found at the psychological level. Hume thought of the mind as a realm of mental states that could be investigated and explained without any reference to the brain. And he thought of mental states ('impressions' and 'ideas') as things, although non-physical ones. On these assumptions, it is natural to answer the question of what unites the experiences of a single stream of consciousness by looking for some kind of psychological thread or mental glue. This is part of a philosophical tradition of thinking about the mind, lasting until the end of the nineteenth century, which supposed that the factors which explain conscious states must themselves be open to introspective observation.

Since we are not tied to that set of assumptions, we can see the unity of consciousness as something probably to be explained at the neurophysiological level. There is a conceptual problem of whether the unity of consciousness can be described in purely impersonal terms, or whether its description has to presuppose the person who has the unified experience. But the *explanation* of it seems a matter of the brain mechanisms it depends on. In the case of the unity of consciousness at one time, those mechanisms are likely to involve the kinds of neural links which are severed in the split brain patients.

[1] David Hume: *A Treatise of Human Nature*, edited by L. A. Selby-Bigge, Oxford, 1888, pages 635–6.

Link-ups
==

Consider the neural links between the two hemispheres. Our present knowledge of these links does not go down to the fine structure. Our picture of the corpus callosum is like a deep sea diver's view of an undersea telephone cable. No doubt this will one day be replaced by something more like a telephone engineer's understanding of the individual strands, of where they are each linked to, and of how the signals are coded.

This knowledge of the fine structure of neural links may enable us to replace them if we wish. We may be able to rebuild the links which have been destroyed in split brain patients, and so re-unite their consciousness. If we cannot regenerate neural tissue, some other way of sending the signals between the hemispheres may be as good. Radio signals between specific points in the different hemispheres, triggering the same nerve impulses that would have resulted from ordinary neural transmission, might serve the purpose. This would then open up the possibility of unity of consciousness being preserved even when the hemispheres were some distance away from each other.

Radio links may also open up a more remarkable possibility. Suppose my two hemispheres are communicating at a distance with each other, and your hemispheres are doing the same thing. It seems conceivable that switching the radio links would result in two unified streams of consciousness, both derived from one hemisphere from each of us.

There is a field for investigation here. We do not know whether this kind of link would be possible. And, if it is possible, we do not know what kinds of merging would be open to us. Perhaps radio links between whole brains would be possible, leading to complete merging, so that one consciousness controlled two bodies. Or perhaps there could be merging of one sense but not another, or else some perceptual merging without joint control of action. If such things happened, the sharp boundaries of our present conception of a person might be replaced by blurred ones.

Merging, if it were possible, might be like an extreme version of marriage. And, if we could plug in and out of each other at will, there would be the equivalent of divorce too. Though the decision would feel different. *We* decide to merge, but *I*, the composite person, decide to divide again. Relationships might be transformed by the understanding that would result from having been merged. And, if merging and dividing became very frequent, the contrast between selfishness and altruism might be blurred. Helping other people requires less generosity if I may later merge with them. There might also be problems of inequalities of power. It would be terrible if you were merged against your will with someone who had a more powerful radio device than you.

Some forms of mystical religion have held out as an ideal the oblivion of the individual mind being merged into the cosmic mind. Part of the appeal of this may be its echo of a common mystical feeling: many people sometimes feel that they themselves are limitless, in some way one with the world as a whole. Romain Rolland, in a letter to Sigmund Freud, called this the 'oceanic' feeling. Freud's suggested explanation of it was that it might be a residue of an infant stage before we have learnt to distinguish between ourselves and the rest of the world. ('Our present I-feeling is, therefore, only a shrunken residue of a much more inclusive – indeed, an all-embracing – feeling which corresponded to a more intimate bond between the I and the world about it.')[2] Something like Freud's speculation, perhaps supplemented by the desire people sometimes have fully to share each other's experiences, might explain the attraction of absorption into the cosmic mind.

If all brains had radio links, something like the mystical ideal might be brought about. But it is not clear what would be so good about this. Perhaps the integrated action of many brains would enable the resulting mind to carry out massive intellectual tasks. But, apart from this, the state of consciousness might not be anything out of the ordinary. We would have replaced a variety of people, often enjoying each other's company, by one lonely mind.

[2] Sigmund Freud: *Civilization and its Discontents*, London, 1930, chapter 1.

Hierarchies of control

===

The delights or horrors of integration with other people are (at least) some way off. At present, neural links serve to integrate the experience of a single person. Hume's thought about the mind below the level of an oyster, with only one kind of sensation, brings out a problem about integration. It is plausible that creatures below oyster level do not have self-consciousness. If a single kind of sensation is not enough to generate self-consciousness, how can adding more experiences do so? Neural links merge different experiences. How does the result go beyond experiences that are more complex but still impersonal?

Part of the answer to this is that the neural networks of the brain obviously do much more than merge experiences. They make possible the development of conceptual thought, so that we can classify the world and ask questions about it. The big difference between us and the oyster is not that we have more experiences, but that we have powers of interpreting them.

Another answer is that we become self-conscious partly through things we do, and one function of neural links is to impose coherence and order on what we do. There is a hierarchy of control which contributes to our idea of the self. Simple movements are embedded in larger sequences of action, with the more complex plan able to override the simpler activity. There are striking examples where a more complex plan can override an inability at the simpler level. One neurological patient was unable to carry out a request to make a fist, but, when asked to demonstrate boxing, was able to do so as part of the sequence.[3] Or, in ordinary life, we all know how a focusing of attention can override other behaviour: how a child in a frenzy of anger and distress can be calmed by becoming absorbed in an interesting conversation. Action, like experience, is not just a series of independent units, but has an organized structure.

Self-consciousness is not just a matter of having a lot of experiences, or having a repertoire of acts we can perform. What else is needed?

[3] Norman Geschwind and Edith Kaplan: A Human Cerebral Disconnexion Syndrome, *Neurology*, 1962.

CHAPTER FIVE

PERSONS AND SELF-CONSCIOUSNESS

... when I consider my self-being, my consciousness and feeling of myself, that taste of myself, of *I* and *me* above and in all things, which is more distinctive than the taste of ale or alum, more distinctive than the smell of walnutleaf or camphor, and is incommunicable by any means to another man (as when I was a child I used to ask myself: What must it be to be someone else?). Nothing else in nature comes near this unspeakable stress of pitch, distinctiveness, and selving, this selfbeing of my own.

GERARD MANLEY HOPKINS: *Comments on the Spiritual Exercises of
St. Ignatius Loyola.*

I shall never forget what I have never revealed to anyone, the phenomenon which accompanied the birth of my consciousness of self and of which I can specify both the place and the time. One morning, as a very young child, I was standing in our front door and was looking over to the wood pile on the left, when suddenly the inner vision 'I am a me' shot down before me like a flash of lightning from the sky, and ever since it has remained with me luminously: at that moment my ego had seen itself for the first time and for ever.

JEAN PAUL RICHTER, quoted in Roderick Chisholm: *The First Person.*

T HE WORD 'PERSON' is one of the most controversial in the language. Consider some of the different views expressed about what a person is.

One common thought is that a human being is a person, while members of other species are not. The reason usually given for this is that our psychology is more complex than that of animals. But the kinds of psychological complexity thought to qualify someone for being a person vary. Harry Frankfurt, for instance, has said that what matters is having second-order desires. Animals want things, but

people also want to have some desires rather than others.[1] Daniel
Dennett has suggested that having a sense of justice is necessary for
being a person, 'to the extent that justice does not reveal itself in the
dealings and interactions of creatures, to that extent they are not
persons'.[2]

This exclusion of anyone completely unjust may seem to draw the
boundary rather narrowly. At the other extreme, the view has been
expressed in the abortion debate that a newly fertilized human egg is
a person. That debate illustrates the way the concept is often shaped
to fit people's values. A widely held view of the abortion issue is that
whether or not a foetus has a right to life depends on whether it is a
person. It is hard to avoid the impression that participants on both
sides of the debate start with an attitude to abortion and then decide
the question of personhood accordingly. One philosopher, Michael
Tooley, is open about this. He gives an account of personhood in
terms of moral considerations, which he takes to be prior to the issue
of whether the foetus is a person.[3]

Perhaps we should expect these disputes over what a person is.
Marcel Mauss suggested that it is an illusion to see our conception of
a person as static.[4] He thought it originated with tribal social roles,
mentioning that *persona* was the Latin word for a mask. He sketched
out an account of how the conception evolved, through the Roman
idea of a person as the bearer of legal rights (so that slaves were not
persons), and through Stoic and Christian ideas of the person having
moral value, to the modern way of thinking of a person mainly as
someone with states of consciousness. Mauss thought our conception
was likely to go on changing. I do not known how far Mauss gives a
correct account of these changes. But, like the abortion debate, a
story of this kind illustrates how what people take to be the special
features of a person may vary with other aspects of their outlook.

Because 'person' is a concept with boundaries that are blurred or
disputed, there may be no satisfactory single answer to the question
'What is a person?' I want to suggest that a prime feature of per-

[1] Harry Frankfurt: Freedom of the Will and the Concept of a Person, *Journal of Philosophy*,
1970.
[2] Daniel Dennett: Conditions of Personhood, in *Brainstorms*, Hassocks, 1979.
[3] Michael Tooley: *Abortion and Infanticide*. Oxford, 1983.
[4] Marcel Mauss: A Category of the Human Mind: The Notion of Person; The Notion of
Self, translated by W. D. Halls, in Michael Carrithers, Steven Collins and Steven Lukes (eds.):
The Category of the Person: Anthropology, Philosophy, History, Cambridge, 1985.

sonhood is self-consciousness. A person is someone who can have thoughts, whose natural expression uses the word 'I'. This seems to capture one central strand in our idea of a person. But, since the concept is disputed, this is a suggested way of using the word, rather than a claim that it is somehow the 'correct' account of it.

On this account, Hume's oyster is not a person. It has no thought 'I am being touched' that rises above an impersonal awareness of a sensation. On the other hand, being a person does not require any moment of illumination of the kind Jean Paul Richter had. (Perhaps Richter knew that *he* was standing in the front door before the flash that came to him.) Self-consciousness does require consciousness and some primitive power of thought. But, provided I-thoughts can be had, it does not matter whether their acquisition was in a sudden conscious moment or through slow, unconscious conceptual growth.

This account leaves open the possibility of degrees of self-consciousness, through there being different kinds of I-thoughts, perhaps grasped to different degrees, with the result that being a person may sometimes be a matter of degree.

You and I both have I-thoughts, but those thoughts belong to two different people because they are not located in the same stream of consciousness. A certain unity of consciousness is required for being a single person. This is why it may be less misleading to think of a split brain patient as two people. But perhaps we should not be too rigid here. In the case of temporary brief divisions, it may raise fewer problems to think of one person than of two.

It is suggested, then, that to be a person is to have a single stream of I-thoughts. We now need to consider the self-consciousness involved in having such thoughts.

CHAPTER SIX

===

THE WORD 'I'

One of the most misleading representational techniques in our language is the use of the word 'I' . . .

LUDWIG WITTGENSTEIN: *Philosophical Remarks.*

'I', in my use of it, always indicates me and only indicates me. 'You', 'she', and 'they' indicate different people at different times. 'I' is like my own shadow; I can never get away from it, as I can get away from your shadow. There is no mystery about this constancy, but I mention it because it seems to endow 'I' with a mystifying uniqueness and adhesiveness.

GILBERT RYLE: *The Concept of Mind.*

A PERSON IS SOMEONE who can think I-thoughts. To say this may seem to explain the vague by the enigmatic. The word 'I' has been a source of philosophical problems, at least since Descartes made its peculiar properties the foundation of his philosophical system.

There are two natural reactions to Descartes' derivation of his own existence from his certainty that he was thinking. One is to see it as some kind of verbal trick. The suspicion is that there must be something wrong with conjuring knowledge about what exists out of the fact that a certain kind of sentence ('I am not now thinking') is paradoxical. The other reaction is to accept that Descartes has shown that one's own present existence is indubitable, but has left us the puzzle of explaining just how this can be so. Either reaction leaves us with the sense that the peculiarities of I-statements need pinning down.

I-statements have three notably idiosyncratic features: their adhesiveness, their elusiveness, and a certain kind of irreducibility.

Adhesiveness
==

The property Ryle called 'adhesiveness' is the one that makes 'I' as inescapable as my own shadow. Think of Descartes noticing that he was doubting. Could he have been wrong about who was doing the doubting? In one way, the answer is obviously yes. He, Descartes, might have suffered from the delusion that he was Montaigne. He might have wrongly or confusedly thought 'I cannot doubt that I, Michel de Montaigne, am doubting.' But is there room for a second kind of mistake about who is doing the doubting? This mistake would be expressed by the thought, 'Someone is doubting, but am *I* the one who is doing it?'

There is no room for this question.[1] Suppose I have a car crash, and wake up in hospital with amnesia and a headache. I have forgotten my name and my past, so I do not know that Jonathan Glover has a headache, and I do not know what kind of person has a headache. But I do know that *I* am having the headache. I cannot think, 'Here is this headache; I hope it is not me who is having it.' And, as Gareth Evans has pointed out, this does not just apply to what we usually classify as mental states. It is equally absurd to say, 'Someone is walking over this bridge; I wonder if it is me?'[2]

The view that our knowledge of the world is based on our experiences, combined with the way 'I' is attached to our experiences, sometimes seems to support solipsism: it can seem that I have a more secure guarantee that the experiences belong to me than that they relate to anything in the world outside.

Elusiveness
==

What *does* 'I' refer to? What are I-thoughts about?

David Hume tried to discover what 'I' refers to by attending to his own experiences, and trying to catch himself having them. He came to the conclusion that the word does not refer to anything,

[1] Ludwig Wittgenstein: *The Blue Book*, in *The Blue and Brown Books*, Oxford, 1958, page 67, and Sydney Shoemaker: Self-Reference and Self-Awareness, *Journal of Philosophy*, 1968.
[2] Gareth Evans: *The Varieties of Reference*, Oxford, 1982, pages 218–219.

apart from the stream of experiences that 'I' am supposed to own. He said,

> For my part, when I enter most intimately into what I call *myself*, I always stumble on some particular perception or other, of heat or cold, light or shade, love or hatred, pain or pleasure. I can never catch *myself* at any time without a perception, and never can observe any thing but the perception.[3]

'I' does not refer to some mental object that can be discovered by introspection. And other philosophers have expressed a more general doubt about what it can refer to. Ludwig Wittgenstein said that the subject that has thoughts does not exist:

> If I wrote a book called *The World as I found it*, I should have to include a report on my body, and should have to say which parts were subordinate to my will, and which were not, etc., this being a method of isolating the subject, or rather of showing that in an important sense there is no subject; for it alone could *not* be mentioned in that book.

He likened this to the way the visual field may contain no clue that it is seen by an eye.[4]

The same elusiveness of 'I' can be brought out by imagining brain transplants. If my brain could be transplanted into your body, and yours transplanted into mine, in which body would *I* be? Perhaps this question does not have a straightforward answer. Imagine a government department located in London. Suppose all the junior officials are moved to Newcastle, while the senior ones stay in London. The question, 'Where is the department?' used to have a clear answer, but now does not.

The parallel with the government department suggests that, in the normal case, where the brain is not relocated, the question, 'Where am I?' does have a clear answer. In a way, this is obviously correct. I am over here in this chair writing this book. In other words, I am where my body is.

But, at a more fine-grained level, the elusiveness reappears. Do I fill the whole of my body? Or are some parts more intimately me than others? Artificial limbs do not raise worries about personal

[3] David Hume: *A Treatise of Human Nature*, edited by L. A. Selby-Bigge, Oxford, 1888, page 252.
[4] Ludwig Wittgenstein: *Tractatus Logico-Philosophicus*, translated by D. F. Pears and B. F. McGuinness, London, 1961, proposition 5.63 ff.

identity. Perhaps any part of my body, except my brain, could be replaced without it being the end of *me*. Perhaps, then, I am my brain? Or, am I only part of my brain? The I is elusive whether we try to find it introspectively, as Hume did, or to pin down its precise physical location.

Irreducibility
==

I see on television the ludicrous 'photofit' picture of the man the police are looking for in connection with the bank robbery. As in the past, I deride the picture: 'That could even be me.' And the same goes for the vague description that is issued: clean-shaven white male in his forties, medium height, overweight, clumsy movements. That could be me too. But this time it *is* me. Some malicious person has given false information to put the police on my trail. It is a tremendous shock finally to realize that *I* am the person they want.

But, however detailed or accurate it is, I do not get a shock until I realize the description is of me. In the same way, hearing the winning lottery number means little until I discover that *I* have that number. In these cases, the statement that I am the person the police want or am the lottery winner cannot be made using only 'neutral' descriptions of me. The word 'I' (or some equivalent, such as 'me') has to be used. There is always a possible gap between the neutral description and what can be conveyed by using 'I'. This is because, however complete the description, I may fail to realize that it refers to me.

Thomas Nagel has suggested that an objective description of the world is bound to leave out something: that, out of all the people in the world, this particular one happens to be me. This (to me) important fact is visible only from my perspective. An objective description can indicate that each person, including Jonathan Glover, has a particular viewpoint from which they see the world. But it cannot mention something I care about: that I *am* Jonathan Glover, and so that perspective is of particular interest to me. (Nagel, whose point this is, makes it in terms of a fact that is of greater interest to him: the fact that he is Thomas Nagel.)

'I' as an indexical

'I' is adhesive, elusive and irreducible. At least part of the explanation of these properties is that it is an indexical: a word which varies in what it refers to according to features of the context in which it is used. (Some other indexicals are 'this', 'here' and 'now'.)

The adhesiveness of 'I' can lead people towards solipsism. That experiences belong to me can seem more certain than that they reflect a world outside me. Ernst Mach said that the solipsist is like the person who never turns round because he would still only see what is in front of him.[5]

Mach's point brings out both a weakness of this case for solipsism and the explanation of the adhesiveness of 'I'. What indexicals refer to depends on context. What makes up 'the scene in front of me' depends on which way I am facing when I refer to it. The place 'here' refers to depends on where the word is spoken. And the time 'now' refers to varies with when the word is used. 'I' is also an indexical, and the person it refers to depends on who is speaking.

The adhesiveness of 'I', as Ryle saw, is matched by the adhesiveness of 'here' and of 'now'. The argument for solipsism based on its adhesiveness is no stronger than arguing from the adhesiveness of 'here' to the conclusion that other places may not exist. If 'I' is inescapable, it is also true that the place I am at is always here, and the time is always now. Tomorrow never comes. The adhesiveness of 'I' is no more mysterious than that.

The elusiveness of 'I' is tied to its being an indexical in two different ways. As with other indexicals, such as 'this', there is not a fixed thing it refers to. The reference varies with the speaker. But this is obviously not the whole story. The elusiveness of 'I' is not just a matter of being uncertain which person is speaking. The question of whether I am my body, my brain, or part of my brain, or a non-physical mind related to my brain, can arise when there is no doubt which person is speaking.

A second feature of some indexicals is relevant. The boundaries of what is referred to may be vague or ambiguous. 'Here' can refer to this room, this house, this town, or this galaxy. It would be ridiculous

[5] Ernst Mach: *The Analysis of Sensation*, New York, 1959, page 359.

to discuss, without specifying a context, where the boundaries of 'here' come. The same is true of 'I'.

The irreducibility of 'I' is also linked to its being an indexical. There is a gap between my understanding a general description of a car and my grasping that it is *this* one. There is a gap between my knowing that the clocks go back on 15 October and knowing that they go back *today*. It is a feature of indexicals, including 'I', that there is room for such failure to connect a non-indexical description with *this* context. 'I' is irreducible in the way other indexicals are. (There is a question whether all indexicals are reducible to the demonstrative 'this', or whether they are mutually interwoven, with none having priority. This issue need not concern us here.)

The flexible reference of 'I'
==

One suggestion, powerfully argued for by G. E. M. Anscombe, is that the word 'I' misleads us because we wrongly think of it as referring to something.[6] She says that, if we think of 'I' as a name, we have to say what kind of thing it names, and this leads to the unhelpful invention of a mysterious 'self'.

An alternative is to think of 'I' as a demonstrative, like 'this' or 'that'. But to understand demonstratives we have to have an answer to the question, 'this what?' In the case of 'I', there seems no exactly parallel question. If there were, the kind of object specified might again have to be something like a 'self'. Also, other demonstratives can fail to refer to anything: I may ask about that figure by the rock, and be mistaken that there is a figure there at all. There seems no equivalent mistake by which 'I' can fail to refer. Professor Anscombe points out that my body cannot be what 'I' always succeeds in referring to, since, in conditions of sensory deprivation, I may be unaware of my body yet still able to think I-thoughts. Interpreting 'I' as a demonstrative which always refers, but not to my body, seems again to leave us with the 'self' as the thing it refers to.

Professor Anscombe thinks we get into these difficulties by assuming that there has to be something 'I' refers to: 'And this is the

[6] G. E. M. Anscombe: The First Person, in S. Guttenplan (ed.): *Mind and Language*, Oxford, 1975.

solution: "I" is neither a name nor another kind of expression whose logical role is to make a reference *at all*.'

The conclusion goes against some of our intuitive thoughts. Take for instance the two sentences, 'I am going to put my foot down about this' (said by Margaret Thatcher) and 'Mrs Thatcher is going to put her foot down about this' (said by someone else). We would naturally suppose that the two sentences referred to the same person. And it would be natural, as part of an account of the use of 'I' in English, to say that it always refers to the person who uses it.

The counter-intuitive conclusion that 'I' does not refer to anything can be avoided. It is right to reject the view that it is a name. But the demonstratives 'this' and 'that' are not the only alternatives. Other indexicals, such as 'here' and 'now', provide a better model. As with 'I', there is no analogous question to 'this what?' And they share the adhesiveness of 'I'.

The indexicals 'here', 'now' and 'I' can all be taken as referring: to a place, a time and a person. All have two kinds of flexibility in what they refer to. The first we have seen: *which* place, time or person they refer to depends respectively on where, when and by whom they are used. The second kind of flexibility is over where their boundaries come. As we have also seen, 'here' can be interpreted narrowly or widely. 'Now' may be interpreted more broadly by a historian making a comparison with medieval life than by a drill instructor. The boundaries of what 'I' refers to may be similarly flexible. In everyday life, there is no problem about where a person's boundaries are. But, if we come across Siamese twins, people with multiple personality, split brain patients, or people with transplanted brains, we may need the flexibility such an indexical allows.

The boundaries may be flexible, but at any particular time we use these words, we have to have *some* idea of their limits. To be told my missing pen is here is little help if the speaker turns out to have had *no* boundaries of 'here' in mind at all. Kant made a similar point about 'I'. To have a conception of myself, I have to have a conception of a frontier between myself and the rest of the world. This conception is central to self-consciousness.

CHAPTER SEVEN

THE
BODY

The I is first and foremost a bodily I.

SIGMUND FREUD: *The Ego and the Id*.

AS A NEW-BORN baby, I may not have known where I stopped and the rest of the world began. This may be something babies have to learn. As Kant stressed, self-consciousness is bound up with awareness of this frontier. If I did not know where the frontier came, it is hard to see what idea I could have of myself as something separate from the rest of the world. As adults we have no difficulty in locating the frontier. It is at the outer surface of the body: where the skin is. This platitude may seem not worth stating. But, in order to understand self-consciousness, it is necessary to take obvious truths and to see how they are explained. It is helpful to bring to this very familiar frontier the curiosity Martian scientists might bring to the investigation of us as an alien form of life. What reasons would a Martian scientist give for placing the boundary of an individual member of the human species where the skin comes?

Some of these reasons appeal to the role of my body as something perceived. When others see or touch me, what they perceive is my body. My body is also something I am aware of. I do not perceive it in the same way others do, and this contributes to my sense that its frontiers are mine.

Other reasons appeal to the role of the body in perceiving other things. Further relevant facts are the special role of the body in action, and in the links between perception and action. The body is not controlled from outside: its control system, the brain, is inside it. The frontiers of the body are sharp rather than fuzzy, and it has a continuous path through space and time. These facts are utterly familiar to us, but their links with the boundaries of a person are sometimes only made clear by imagining how things might have been different.

Take first the way people perceive each other. To see someone is to see a body. And bodies tell us a lot about people. We learn about their age, their sex, and perhaps their race, something about their strength, their state of health and their weight. We learn about their attractiveness, and we can see something of how they think of themselves and how they want to be seen. From their posture and from their style of bodily movement we may get an impression of their mood or even of their job.

The face

Most of all, we can read faces. We use the face as the main way of recognizing people. One clue to how far members of a species are self-conscious is facial recognition. Chimpanzees looking in a mirror can tell their own faces from those of other chimpanzees. And people suffering from the psychiatric disorder of 'depersonalization' sometimes find that, while their face in a mirror looks familiar, it does not seem to belong to them. Reading faces is sufficiently important to have its own brain mechanism. Brain damage can cause prosopagnosia, the inability to recognize faces, despite being able to see things in the ordinary way, and despite normal ability to recognize everything else.

Faces are not just recognized. We also interpret them. We can often tell what people are looking at, or even thinking about, and what their reaction or emotional state is. We think we can learn more from a face than just about a person's present state. We make generalizations about character: someone's face shows that they are proud, their eyes show they are kind or cold, or they look serious or compassionate. Sometimes a face may seem to reflect the experiences of years, and the emotions and understanding that have been shaped by them. (Rembrandt self-portraits.)

What we see in Rembrandt's face is surely not all illusory. These paintings are of course a special case: we are looking at an extremely perceptive man, honestly portrayed by a brilliant painter who knows him from the inside. And when, partly taught by Rembrandt, we see other faces in a similar way, we learn things about those people too.

But these judgments of character may not always be reliable. Partly, we may be projecting on to faces things about people known independently. 'His face was all intelligence', said Sir Roy Harrod of J. M. Keynes. It is interesting to speculate what Harrod would have seen in that face if Keynes had been a pilot who specialized in stunt-flying.

Marcel Proust describes this process of projection:

Even the simple act which we describe as 'seeing someone we know' is to some extent an intellectual process. We pack the physical outline of the person we see with all the notions we have already formed about him, and in the total picture of him which we compose in our minds those notions have certainly the principal place. In the end they come to fill out so completely the curve of his cheeks, to follow so exactly the line of his nose, they blend so harmoniously in the sound of his voice as if it were no more than a transparent envelope, that each time we see the face or hear the voice it is these notions which we recognize and to which we listen.[1]

The family of Proust's narrator do not have the same view of their friend Swann as do those who know of his social prominence:

From the Swann they had constructed for themselves my family had left out, in their ignorance, a whole host of details of his life in the world of fashion, details which caused other people, when they met him, to see all the Graces enthroned in his face and stopping at the line of his aquiline nose as at a natural frontier . . .

The narrator's family knew only 'this face divested of all glamour, vacant and roomy as an untenanted house', which they filled with associations drawn from Swann's weekend visits to them.

Sometimes we project things that are not really there on to a face. (But some 'projections' may not be far out. General Pinochet is quoted as saying, 'I am not a dictator. I just have a grumpy face.')[2]

We are aware of what our own faces look like. How my face looks to me (together with the resulting expectation of how it will appear to others) can have a great effect on my sense of my own identity. This comes out clearly in cases of visible damage:

[1] Marcel Proust: *Remembrance of Things Past*, translated by C. K. Scott Moncrieff and Terence Kilmartin, London, 1981, volume 1, page 20.
[2] Quoted in the *Observer*, 11 May 1986.

When I got up at last . . . and had learned to walk again, one day I took a hand glass and went to a long mirror to look at myself, and I went alone. I didn't want anyone . . . to know how I felt when I saw myself for the first time. But there was no noise, no outcry; I didn't scream with rage when I saw myself. I just felt numb. That person in the mirror *couldn't* be me. Yet when I turned my face to the mirror there were my own eyes looking back, hot with shame . . .

I felt as if it had nothing to do with me; it was only a disguise. But it was not the kind of disguise which is put on voluntarily by the person who wears it, and which is intended to confuse other people as to one's identity. My disguise had been put on me without my consent or knowledge like the ones in fairy tales, and it was I myself who was confused by it, as to my own identity. I looked in the mirror, and was horror-struck because I did not recognize myself.[3]

Severe facial disfigurement is rightly regarded as a handicap, to be given surgical help where possible. This is partly because of the reactions it arouses in others, often one of the worst drawbacks of any handicap: 'My face is what separates me from the rest of humanity.'[4] It is partly a handicap because we think of ourselves in terms of the face we are used to, so that a damaged face damages our sense of ourselves. It is also partly because, although facial disfigurement need not impair perception, speech, or the movements used in getting about, it can severely impair our ability to communicate.

Facial expression is a mixture of the natural and the voluntary, and both aspects convey things to others. A lot can be learnt from involuntary facial responses: blushing, a guilty look, or an evasiveness of the eye. And also we use our faces to express things, through eye meets, smiles, frowns and many other kinds of signal. Most animals have a flat facial muscle: only humans and apes have the flexibility and expressiveness given by many different muscles. This subtle vocabulary of expression is superimposed on contours that are natural but individual. So facial expression is doubly distinctive of ourselves.

The role of the body in perception
==

The single body that is mine contains all the sensory systems I use to perceive things. The visual, tactile, auditory and other input I rely on

[3] K. B. Hathaway: *The Little Locksmith*, New York, 1943, quoted in Erving Goffman: *Stigma, Notes on the Management of Spoiled Identity*, Harmondsworth, 1968.
[4] A patient, quoted in Frances Cooke MacGregor: *Transformation and Identity, The Face and Plastic Surgery*, New York, 1974.

are all mediated by the apparatus of the same body. This may again seem too obvious to be worth saying: of course I do not see with your eyes, or feel things with someone else's hands. But again it is worth seeing how the obvious might have been different.

P. F. Strawson has illustrated this with respect to vision.[5] He imagines a case where someone's visual experience depends, not on a single body, but on three. It depends on body A's eyes working properly: sight is stopped by A's eyelids being closed, and damage to A's eyes can impair it. But the angle of vision depends on the direction in which the head and eyeballs of body B are turned. And the place from which the world is seen depends on where body C is.

Imaginary cases where perception depends on more than one body can be thought of in terms of radio links between points in the nervous systems of the different bodies. The mechanisms of Strawson's particular case seem hard to envisage in any detail. When A's eyelids close, we can think of a signal blocking a pathway in the nervous system of B or C. But when B's head and eyeballs rotate, by what mechanism could this alter the angle from which the scene near C is viewed, without altering C's orientation? To get a clear picture of what is happening, we need answers to questions of this sort, as well as having knowledge of which body's visual cortex was involved.

The thought experiment is only rather vaguely sketched out, but Strawson's general point is unaffected. The visual systems of more than one body could be linked in such a way that both were needed for sight to occur. This could equally be true of auditory or other sensory systems. And radio links would also make it possible for, say, the visual, tactile and auditory systems feeding in to one brain to be located each in a different body. So, when we say that in actual human beings the sensory apparatus is all located in a single body, we are saying that various imaginable forms of perception are not ours. The Martian scientist, perhaps more aware of these alternatives than we are, may give this fact about our perception as one of his reasons for treating the boundaries of a single body as the boundaries of a human being.

[5] P. F. Strawson: *Individuals*, London, 1959, chapter 3.

The role of the body in action
==

A high degree of consciousness might have evolved in beings rooted to the spot like trees. But the human body moves about. It has a continuous path through space and time, which could be tracked by a camera. The film would show no gaps, no disappearances followed by re-appearances. If there were such gaps, there would be a problem of whether the person after the gap was the same as the person before the gap or just a replica. The human body does not divide like an amoeba. If it did, there would be a problem of whether either or both of the resulting people were the same as the person before the division. This would blur our picture of the body as having a persisting unity. And the body is not like a swarm of bees whose members can go off in different directions. It is natural to treat the body as a unit because it moves about as one.

My body is also marked off from other things by the fact that there is nothing else I can act on in the same immediate way. If I want a table to move I have to give it a shove with my arms. But when I want my arms to do this, I do not have to give them a shove. It is again possible to imagine things being different. If signals could be sent from my nervous system to receptors in physical objects detached from my body, so that I could move those objects in the same direct way that I can move my arms, it might be less clear that I stop where my body ends. These doubts would be even stronger if sensory signals could be sent back enabling me to 'feel' things happening in the detached objects. We might then say that I extend beyond my body, or else we might treat these objects as free-floating parts of my body.

Some neurological patients have to cope with loss of direct control over parts of the body normally subject to it. An aspect of the body over which control is lost or impaired can start to seem like something external to be manipulated, rather than part of me. In cases where the limbs are working, and the defect is in some higher-level control system, a subtle psychology of self-manipulation can be developed. Ivan Vaughan has described his strategies during his morning run for resisting his severe Parkinsonian tremor:

A problem may arise if someone else comes on the scene just at the point where I am wanting to walk for a bit, as the tremor will manifest itself quite vigorously. As the person approaches, emotions build up and I find myself stooping further forward. So I break out into a run in order to pass the person without exhibiting tremor.[6]

The external context can impede or smooth the path of action. Ivan Vaughan gives an instance:

There is a crossing with loud beeps at frequent intervals when the time is right to cross. I avoid using this and prefer to jay-walk, both because the beeps set off a deadline and because the cars are brought to a standstill and the occupants simply sit and watch me as I walk in front of them.

Dr Oliver Sacks says that some of his patients with Parkinson's disease can have their movement problems eased by music. They are even helped by smooth curves, rather than sharp corners, in the paths and passages they walk along. Sacks describes some of their strategies of 'external' manipulation of action:

Hester's tendency to walk too fast was moderated if she had to walk *uphill* (as it was aggravated if she had to walk *downhill*); it was also moderated if she *thought* she was walking uphill . . . She once asked me if it might not be possible to make a special pair of glasses for her which would distort appearances so that all the level corridors would seem to her to be going uphill.[7]

When control of part of the body is impaired, there is a tendency for the perceived boundaries of the self to shrink to exclude the recalcitrant part. Only a tendency: there are the countervailing pressures of our whole normal way of thinking, together with the sensory input from the affected region. The tendency is illustrated in some things Raymond Aron said about his experience of having a stroke:

In the space of a second I had become an onlooker, a spectator of my body and my crippled speech; and my *I*, my self, my 'soul' was holding out in spite of everything, apparently intact (an illusion of course) . . .

Mon *je*, my *I*, had abruptly taken up residence outside my body and was wondering, with more curiosity than serenity, what instruments it had at its disposal . . .

What I saw, a few weeks after the shock, as accounting for my behaviour was the complete continuity of my awareness, of my 'I', my conscious *je*. My brain had been damaged, not myself. My speech centre had suffered impairment, not

---

[6] Ivan Vaughan: Learning the Tactics of Coping, *The Listener*, December, 1984.
[7] Oliver Sacks: *Awakenings*, Harmondsworth, 1976, page 320.

my thought centre; my right hand had become awkward, but the flaw in the instrument did not affect the workman.[8]

Such cases of impairment tell us about our normal state. It is because most of us have unhampered direct control over so many bodily movements that we have no tendency to contract the self inward from the bodily boundary. The Martian scientist, describing the contribution of this control to the bodily frontier of the self, might add another factor: control of a single body is normally not shared. I do not find that my decision to walk across the room comes into conflict with some alien decision that my body will stay sitting down. If I did, this body might start to seem less like home territory, and more like territory that I was disputing with someone else. In the cases that do resemble this (split brain patients and cases of multiple personality) we are less confident that one body corresponds to one person.

Links between perception and action
==

The body whose movements I can control directly is the same one whose sensory apparatus is used in my perception of things. (It is also relevant that the brain which integrates this is located inside the body, rather than linked to it from outside.) These two kinds of bodily function interact in obvious ways. Perceptual feedback is used to control and guide action. (This is obvious in the case of vision, but applies to other senses too. Local anaesthetics, affecting tactile feedback, can distort movement as well.) And movements play a part in perception, letting me feel a surface or see something from a different angle.

Are these links between the movements and sensory processes of a single body merely contingent: features which the Martian scientist may note that we happen to have? Or are they inevitable features of any self-conscious being? Stuart Hampshire has argued that it is not a contingent matter of fact that my experiences change as I move, or that through control of my body I can switch my observation from one thing to another. He says,

If one tries to imagine a kind of perception that does not conform to these conditions, and in which the body of the observer, movable at will, is not the

[8] Raymond Aron: The Stroke – A Memoir Before the End, *Encounter*, February, 1984.

medium of perception, one finds that the distinction between the perceiver and the object of perception has altogether disappeared.[9]

Hampshire's argument for this appeals to how I draw the frontier between myself and the rest of the world. Things outside us are seen from different angles as we move about. Sensations internal to us cannot be varied in this way: I cannot vary the angle from which an itch or a headache is perceived. Hampshire also emphasizes the felt resistance of physical objects to my intentional movements:

I find my power of movement limited by the resistances of objects around me. This felt resistance to my will defines for me, in conjunction with my perceptions, my own situation as an object among other objects.

It is surely plausible that movement, in both these ways, helps to establish my frontiers. But perhaps it is an exaggeration to suggest that, without this information, the distinction between me and what I perceive altogether disappears. A person paralysed from birth might get some idea of his frontiers by noting that tactile sensations were experienced when parts of what we would identify as his body were touched, but not when things came into contact with his bed or the wall. Also, it may not be necessary for information about how things look from different angles to come from movements under my voluntary control. The paralysed person whose bed was wheeled about might get the same knowledge.

Perhaps intentional movement is theoretically dispensable for self-consciousness. But, as things are, the role played by a single body in the interplay between perception and movement is another reason for saying that I stop where my body does.

Sharp boundaries

==

There could be forms of consciousness located in bodies far less sharply marked off from each other than are the bodies of different human beings. We are familiar with blurred boundaries in rare cases such as Siamese twins. But fuzzy boundaries could be the norm for a species. Imagine brains dotted around in a mass of jelly. Each brain

[9] Stuart Hampshire: *Thought and Action*, London, 1959, chapter 1.

can wobble the jelly close to it. The area it can wobble varies, being quite large on 'good' days and severely contracted on 'bad' ones. Each brain is also sensitive to the jelly near it being touched. The area to which it is sensitive again expands and contracts, though in a way that does not correlate with variations in the scope of its active power. Sometimes a region of jelly can be 'felt' by more than one brain. Sometimes it can be acted on by more than one brain. And sometimes it will be within the zone of sensitivity of one and within the sphere of activity of another.

Our bodies, unlike the brains in jelly, have clear and constant boundaries. (The constancy of a boundary is important. Life would be harder for patriots in a world where national boundaries shifted with the seasons.) And the scope of our bodily sensitivity coincides at the edges with the domain of our direct control over movement.

My body perceived

Even when no mirror is around, part of the body is often visible. While reading this, you can probably see your hands holding the book. Some psychologists have argued that seeing our own bodies plays a part in visual perception of the rest of the world. J. J. Gibson, for instance, has suggested a role for the glimpse of our nose at the bottom of the visual field. Perception of how far away things are is based partly on the degree of disparity between what is presented to the two eyes. The nose may provide a baseline for comparison here. It may similarly give a baseline for estimates of the relative size and motion of things.[10]

In general, sight tells us less about ourselves than about others. But I am aware of my body in ways not available to other people. I feel my body being touched. I feel bodily pain and pleasure; I feel sick, and so on. Perhaps most important is my proprioceptive sense: I feel the position and movement of my limbs. If this sense fails, as it did in Oliver Sacks's patient Christina, there can be a terrible feeling of disembodiment and a desire for reassurance. Christina liked open cars: 'I feel the wind on my arms and face, and then I know, faintly, I

[10] J. J. Gibson: *The Ecological Approach to Visual Perception*, Boston, 1979, chapter 7.

have arms and a face. It's not the real thing, but it's something – it lifts this horrible, dead veil for a while.'[11]

Proprioception may be influenced by other sensory information, for instance by what we see. Gibson describes a device called 'The Haunted Swing'. In what appears to be a room, a swing is set up on a bar. You sit on the swing and it appears to move. But really, the swing is still and the 'room' is moving. This misleading visual impression generates bodily feelings of movement.[12]

Perhaps feelings of bodily states underlie the claims of some people to be aware, not only of their thoughts, but also of the 'self' that is having the thoughts. William James said that when he thought in visual terms, or remembered things, he had sensations in his eyeballs. He said that agreeing, disagreeing, or making a mental effort, involved sensations in the throat. He concluded that, 'in one person at least, *the "Self of selves", when carefully examined, is found to consist mainly of the collection of these peculiar motions in the head or between the head and throat.*'[13]

Obviously it is not plausible to say that *I* am a cluster of sensations in the head and throat. But if these sensations accompany a lot of our mental activity, they may seem to be a medium in which the activity takes place. Awareness of them could give the illusion of being aware of the I which Hume failed to find. We all respond to Gerard Manley Hopkins's reference to the taste of himself, more distinctive than the taste of ale or alum. But perhaps it is the poverty of our vocabulary for describing bodily sensations that makes them seem incommunicable to others, and so generates an illusion of uniqueness. (We project debatable interpretations, not only on to the appearance of others, but even on to our own bodily sensations.)

Disorders of body image

The bodily frontier is my frontier. But, in some pathological cases, notably where the parietal lobe is damaged, awareness of this frontier

---

[11] Oliver Sacks: *The Man Who Mistook His Wife for a Hat*, London, 1985, page 51.

[12] J. J. Gibson: loc. cit.

[13] William James: *The Principles of Psychology*, New York, 1890, volume 1, page 301.

can become confused. The frontier as perceived, the subjective frontier, no longer coincides with the objective one.

This is illustrated by 'unilateral neglect'.[14] A patient with parietal damage may be asked, 'Put out your hands,' or, 'Put on these slippers.' Only one hand moves, though the other may move when this is pointed out. Only one slipper is put on. The defect is not muscular, since activities using both sides of the body in coordination, such as walking or typing, are unimpaired. In later stages of the disorder, only one side of the person's hair is combed, or only one side of the face is shaved. Looking in a mirror does not correct this. It seems that half the body is simply not recognized as part of me. This, rather than inability to move, is the problem. When the person with the disorder is asked to put on gloves, only one glove is put on, but the 'neglected' hand is used to do this.

Other distortions of body image include the appearance of a phantom third hand. In some cases this is 'seen' as well as 'felt'. Sometimes parts of the body seem distorted, separated or torn. Sometimes there is the feeling that the whole body has disappeared or rotted away.

Some patients are unaware that half their body is paralysed, and produce confabulations to explain away evidence of the paralysis. Shown the arm they cannot move, they may deny its existence. Or they may give bizarre accounts of mechanical interventions preventing its movement. Or they may deny that it is theirs, sometimes naming someone else as its owner. One male patient is reported to have had erotic sensations, aroused by his own left side, which he thought belonged to a woman beside him. In other cases, there is something less than belief. There is rather what neurologists call an 'aura': it feels as if my hand belongs to someone else, or I have an inclination to imagine that someone else's limbs are mine. Perhaps the best model for thinking of auras is the déjà vu experience. We feel that we have been here or done this before, without accepting the feeling as reliable.

Some of the problems of interpreting these body image disorders arise from the difficulty of getting a clear account of what the experience is like. As those with these disorders often have more general brain decay or damage, they are likely to be confused. But there are more theoretical difficulties as well.

Our picture of someone's beliefs is always interwoven with our

[14] MacDonald Critchley: *The Parietal Lobe*, London, 1953, chapter 8.

picture of their other mental states. Our evidence about their beliefs is partly what they say, but our interpretation of this depends on our view of their sincerity. Our evidence is based partly on their actions. But how we interpret their actions depends on what we think they want to do or are able to do. We revise our picture to keep the person's behaviour coherent and intelligible. Detective stories are full of these revisions, both by the detective and by the reader. The story seems unconvincing if, when the murderer is discovered, we have no coherent account of why some of the other suspects were prowling about on the night.

Coherence is central to our everyday understanding of people. But it breaks down in some neurological disorders, causing special problems in interpreting them. In body image disorders, we cannot be quite sure what is perceived or believed, as some of the usual connections between perception, belief and action have broken down.

There are also the usual problems in interpreting confabulation, which may be anything between unconsciously filling in a gap and the conscious invention of a story to avoid a discrepancy being detected. There are further problems of distinguishing auras from full-blown false beliefs.

Other problems arise from the vague term 'body image'. There are at least three different things it may refer to. There is the visual image we have of our body. There is a tactile image of the body: how my body feels when I shut my eyes and pay attention to it. And there is my awareness of my size, shape and posture. This awareness is not just a matter of sensations, although they may contribute to it. Brian O'Shaughnessy likens this aspect of body image to a bus driver's feel for a bus. The equivalent of body image is not to have sensations or mental images, but to know where the bus will fit.[15]

These different kinds of body image need not be a unity, and perhaps some of the distortions involve interference with one and not another. What the disorders have in common is that some kind of subjective frontier diverges from the normal bodily frontier. But we do not have to accept that any real boundary has shifted.

'I' functions like 'here' in the flexibility of what it refers to. So we *can* contract the boundaries of 'I' to fit a subjective contraction in these cases. But to do so does not undermine the more normal way

---

[15] Brian O'Shaughnessy: *The Will*, Cambridge, 1980.

of drawing the boundary. (And sometimes the flexibility of 'I' would be strained by following the subjective frontier. It would be odd to say my arm is part of you because parietal damage makes you think it is.) Even where the subjective boundary has shifted, it is still reasonable to see the bodily frontier as the objective one.

CHAPTER EIGHT

AM I MY BODY?

> But O alas, so long, so farre
> Our bodies why doe wee forbeare?
> They are ours, though they are not wee, wee are
> The intelligences, they the spheare.
>
> JOHN DONNE: 'The Extasie'.

And our bodies themselves, are they simply ours, or are they *us*?

WILLIAM JAMES: *The Principles of Psychology*.

MY FRONTIERS ARE those of my body. I may be unconscious for periods, but I still exist: my body has a continuous path through space and time. It is what is perceived by others when they perceive me. And the special ways in which I am aware of my body are at least a large part of my own self-consciousness. Should I then stop thinking of my body as mine and think of it as me?

My corpse is not me. The view worth considering is that I am my living body. Perhaps a further modification is needed to allow for the case where a body is alive, but where the brain will never again function in the way needed for consciousness. If irreversible loss of consciousness is the end of me, the view that I am my body will have to stipulate that my body must be both alive and capable of consciousness.

The two issues this raises turn out to be related. The first is whether all parts of my body are essential to *my* existence. The second is whether saying that I am my body allows an adequate role for my mental life.

Is my whole body essential to me?
===

There is a complication raised by transplants. If my kidney or heart
fails, I shall be glad to have a transplant. My only worry will be
whether it will work. But if the neurologist says my brain is functioning poorly, I shall be far less reassured by the offer of a brain
transplant. I may feel, not that I am being given someone else's
brain, but that someone else is being given my body. My brain
seems more essential to *me* than is the rest of my body.

This has led some philosophers to the view that I am my brain.[1]
But, once my frontiers are narrowed to the brain, it is hard to stop
there. Are all parts of the brain essential to me? It is hard to see why
the mechanisms in the cerebellum which control breathing are so
different from the heart or the lungs. Some strong arguments would
be needed to show that, while *I* survive a heart transplant, I could
not survive the replacement of the cerebellar breathing mechanisms.
The brain is singled out because of its contribution to mental life. It
is hard to see why its other functions are more relevant than those of
the rest of the body.

But, once we move in from the frontier between brain and body,
it is again hard to know where to stop. If removing a brain tumour
destroys a mechanism used in doing multiplication, is it clear that the
resulting person is no longer me? Any attempt to mark off a physical
region, whether the whole brain or part of it, seems doomed to
arbitrariness.

The flexible reference of the word 'I' can be invoked. Just as 'here'
can refer to this room or to this country, so the limits of 'I' are
usually set by the bodily frontier, but, in rare cases, such as brain
transplants, they can be set more narrowly. It is open to someone to
say that I am my body, while allowing that I may survive the
destruction of some bits of it and not others. But, on this approach,
there are essential and inessential bodily parts of me, and the essential
parts are those most closely bound up with my mind.

---

[1] Thomas Nagel: *The View From Nowhere*, Oxford, 1986, chapter 3.

My mental life
==

The special role of the brain brings out a deeper problem for the view that I am my body. The brain is special because of its role in my mental life, particularly my conscious life. This is crucial to me: it is very dubious that *I* am still there when in irreversible coma. So it is only plausible that I am my body if my mental life is reducible to the functioning of my brain. Many deny that it is. They say that there is more to people than can be described in physical or in functional terms.

The background to this is the way an old dualist model of the mind has been replaced in the neurosciences.

The traditional dualist picture of human beings assumed interaction between mind and body. On this picture, what goes on when I see a ball and catch it involves the interaction between physical and non-physical processes. Light strikes my retina, which causes nerve impulses to be sent up the optic nerve and eventually to the visual cortex. This causes me to have a visual experience (itself a mental event, not physically located in the brain or anywhere else). The visual experience causes me to decide to catch the ball. This decision is another purely mental event, which, in turn, causes physical events in the brain, which send nerve impulses causing my muscles to move.

Ever since Descartes championed this model, people have felt puzzled about it. What can be said about the nature of these mental events? How is the interaction with the brain supposed to work?

In recent years, neuroscientists have hoped to avoid all this by explaining mental activity entirely in terms of brain mechanisms. The assumption has been that mental states will be reducible to states of the brain. Supporters of the old interactionist model have to bet on the neurosciences failing to carry out this programme. It is not certain to succeed, but progress so far has put dualism on the defensive.

This alternative to dualism does not deny that people have experiences. So, to accept it we do not have to 'pretend to be anaesthetized', as A. J. Ayer once said of behaviourists. But the account of our experiences is reductionist: there is no role for any states or events without physical embodiment. Experiences are thought of as *being* states of the brain. Or, in the version known as functionalism, they have the same relation to brain states that the functional states of a computer have to its physical states.

Functionalism is the most sophisticated attempt so far to give a non-dualist account of the mind. Two different kinds of computer can be in the same functional state (going through the same stages in working out the same mathematical problem) but, because of their different design, their physical states may be different. The computer's 'mental' states are its functional states, not its physical ones. But this does not mean that any mysterious interaction between the physical and the non-physical is needed to explain its operation.

Applied to people, this account says that our mental states are the functional states of our brains. This allows for the possibility that your brain may operate differently from mine, with different neurons firing when we are having the same experiences. It allows the possibility of consciousness in animals with different brains from ours. It also allows that consciousness may be present in beings made of quite different material from us. So it allows for Martian or robot consciousness.

Despite the theoretical appeal of functionalism, many people have a deep intuitive resistance to it. This often takes the form of a rather inarticulate feeling that this cannot be the whole story about us. Recent work in philosophy has helped to make the central objection more articulate. It has to do with the 'subjectivity' of experience. It can be brought out by two questions, one about robots, and one about blind people.

Suppose we construct a robot whose 'brain' functions just like ours, although it consists of silicon chip. Its exterior, as in science fiction films, is metallic. But, unlike any present robots, its behaviour passes any test for consciousness that we do. It does not just play chess, but appears also to read novels, fall in love, daydream, and enjoy jokes. It can take part in a sophisticated conversation about whether its present feeling is shame or embarrassment.

Should we say that the robot really has experiences, or just that it behaves as though it does? Its behaviour gives us more evidence in favour of its consciousness than we have in the case of cats or monkeys. Against this, there is the argument that since it is not alive it is not conscious. But perhaps restricting consciousness to things made of the same sort of stuff as us is just a prejudice. (Imagine

Martians, who like to boil us alive before eating us. They wonder if this is cruel, but are reassured by the thought that we only behave as though conscious. Nothing made of that weird flabby stuff could actually *be* conscious.)

Our problem with the robots is that they are like us in behaviour, but unlike us in composition. And there seems no obvious way of deciding which feature is the relevant one. The functionalist has an answer: these robots are conscious because their functional states are the same as ours. But we are left with the uneasy feeling that either answer may be wrong.

Since no evidence looks conclusive either way, can we just *choose* which criteria to use? This too may leave us uneasy. Imagine the Martians choosing criteria according to which we are not conscious. Such a decision is not one that settles the matter, since it can be wrong. Those who share these worries may feel that knowing the functional states of a robot does not settle whether it has experiences.

A similar issue can be raised by considering people born blind. Suppose that one of them becomes a physiologist, and specializes in the functioning of the visual system. (Imagine this is in a hundred years' time, when its functioning is fully understood.) Does the blind physiologist know all there is to know about the experience of seeing? Or is it possible that such a physiologist, after having sight restored by an operation, might say, 'I had no idea colours would look like that'? Perhaps there is something about seeing that the physiologist knows now but did not know before. In this case, as in that of the robots, there seems to be something about experience that eludes description in functional terms.[2]

The question of whether functionalism is a correct account of the mind is not yet resolved. Whether it can satisfactorily accommodate subjectivity is still disputed. To deny that it can is to have a reason for thinking mental states may transcend anything physical. This leads people to think that I am not reducible to my body, or even to part of it, such as my brain.

My identity is obviously rooted in the continuous existence of my body. And my mental life is identified as *mine* because of its dependence on my brain. But perhaps we should be cautious about going further and saying that *I* am reducible to any set of my physical features.

[2] Ibid., chapter 2.

CHAPTER NINE

====

THE
EGO

I am not thought, I am not action, I am not feeling; I am something that thinks and acts and suffers.

THOMAS REID: *Essays*

But it still appears – and I cannot stop thinking this – that the corporeal things of which images are formed in my thought, and which the senses investigate, are known with much more distinctness than this puzzling 'I' which cannot be pictured in the imagination.

RENÉ DESCARTES: *Meditations*.

It thinks: but that this 'it' is precisely that famous old 'I' is, to put it mildly, only an assumption, an assertion, above all not an 'immediate certainty'.

... and perhaps we and the logicians as well will one day accustom ourselves to getting along without that little 'it' (which is what the honest old 'I' has evaporated into).

FRIEDRICH NIETZSCHE: *Beyond Good and Evil*.

A PERSON IS SOMEONE who has the self-conscious thoughts expressed by using 'I'.

What are these thoughts about? 'I' crops up all the time. I am walking down the street; I am looking at the houses; I am feeling cold; I am annoyed with myself because I was so inarticulate in a discussion yesterday. But what is this 'I' that does these things and has these experiences? It is natural to believe that these experiences and actions belong to me. Part of this is the idea that there is more to *my* having experiences than just a sequence of experiences taking place, more to *my* raising my arm than just my arm going up. But when we try to say anything about the I that makes the difference, we find it hard.

Reductionism denies that 'I' refers to a separate owner of my experiences. One version says I am reducible to my physical character-istics. We have seen some problems for this view.

Another reductionist approach is Hume's. The 'owner' is reduced to the stream of experiences. This clashes with some deep intuitive convictions. It is natural to believe that, although I have had one set of experiences, I could have had a quite different set: I could have taken a different job in another country, but the resulting experiences would still have been *mine*. This line of thought seems hard to reconcile with the view that I am just a particular set of experiences.

Doubts about the first kind of reductionism may make it seem that I am detachable from any particular set of physical properties. Doubts about Hume's version may suggest that I am detachable from any particular set of my mental properties. Together, they may suggest that 'I' refers to something which owns both sets of prop-erties, while not being reducible to either.

This suggestion was given its classic expression by Descartes. He thought that 'I' refers to a thinking mind, inseparable from a particular body but not reducible to it, and which has experiences and thoughts without being reducible to them: 'I am, then, in the strict sense only a thing that thinks; that is, I am a mind, or intelligence, or intellect, or reason – words whose meaning I have been ignorant of until now. But for all that I am a thing which is real and which truly exists.'[1]

A variant of this Cartesian ego is the 'noumenal' self, believed in by Kant. ('Noumenal' denotes things whose existence can be known to us, but about which we can know nothing else, since they have no observable properties.) Kant thought that Descartes was wrong, in his proof of his own existence, to suppose that our stream of conscious-ness tells us anything about our self as it really is. Criticizing Des-cartes, he wrote, 'We must also recognize, as regards inner sense, that by means of it we intuit ourselves only as we are inwardly affected *by ourselves*; in other words, that, so far as inner intuition is concerned, we know our own subject only as appearance, not as it is in itself.'[2] Thinking that 'I' refers to a self whose own nature is unknowable, he at one point rather mysteriously alludes to 'the being which thinks in us'.[3]

---

[1] René Descartes, Second Meditation, in *The Philosophical Writings of Descartes*, translated by John Cottingham, Robert Stoothoff and Dugald Murdoch, Cambridge, 1984, vol. 2, page 59.
[2] Immanuel Kant: *Critique of Pure Reason*, translated by Norman Kemp Smith, London, 1929, B 156.
[3] Ibid., A 401.

(William James approached this with a refreshing briskness: 'The Ego is simply *nothing*: as ineffectual and windy an abortion as Philosophy can show. It would indeed be one of Reason's tragedies if the good Kant, with all his honesty and strenuous pains, should have deemed this conception an important outbirth of his thought.') [4]

What Descartes and Kant have in common is the belief that 'I' refers to a self, or ego, that is not reducible to anything bodily, or to my experiences, or to any combination of the two. Despite the elaborate expression Kant gave to this idea, it is not just a philosophers' theory. It is a view which many people are almost unconsciously inclined to hold. It obviously has something in common with belief in the soul, found in Christianity and other religions. In the versions of Christianity that do not include the resurrection of the body, the soul is needed as the bearer of immortal life. But belief in the ego can arise out of aspects of our experience which have nothing to do with either philosophy or religion. It is a belief that comes to us very naturally, and it may be that the soul, the Cartesian ego and the noumenal self arise from a common origin.

What makes it natural to think that my physical and mental history are mine but not me?

It is worth separating some of the different origins of this widespread belief in the ego. Some of the reasons are worth taking seriously, while others are offered more in the spirit of diagnosing the irrational causes of the belief.

The roots of the belief are found in our language, in the way we think of our own life history, in the way we think of our own body and of our mental states, in our experience of perceiving things and of acting, and in the unity of our experience.

Language

There is a strong tendency to suppose that words are names of things, and that words in different grammatical categories name things of different types.

Naively, we think verbs name things we do, like running. This leads to problems when applied to verbs like 'to exist', since existing

[4] William James: *The Principles of Psychology*, New York, 1890, volume 1, page 365.

is at best an odd sort of activity. (J. L. Austin once wondered if it was supposed to be 'like breathing, only quieter'.) We have a similar tendency to think of adjectives as names of properties of things, as an apple has the properties of being large, red, round and sour. This leads to the invention of odd sorts of properties to fit adjectives like 'right' and 'wrong', 'delicious' and 'disgusting'. 'Wrongness' and 'disgustingness' are at best properties of peculiar kinds.

The same tendency inclines us to think of nouns and pronouns as words referring to objects. But, as we have seen, if we ask what object is named by 'I', the answer is elusive. If I think that I could have had very different physical characteristics, this may make me reluctant to say that 'I' refers to my body. If I think I could have had a quite different life, I may also be reluctant to accept Hume's belief that 'I' refers to the particular history of experiences I have had. The fact that I-statements are not reducible to statements without indexicals may increase my reluctance to accept either of these reductionist views. And if I resist both of them, but think that there must be something that 'I' refers to, I may be tempted to believe in an ego that owns both my body and my experiences.

And the adhesiveness of 'I' may suggest that it refers to some persisting thing that never slips out of consciousness. When we use 'I', we do not use physical characteristics to identify the person referred to. Wittgenstein suggested that this creates the impression that 'I' refers to 'something bodiless, which, however, has its seat in our body'.[5]

This is reinforced by an illusion to do with the adhesiveness of 'I'. We are inclined, wrongly, to think the adhesiveness of 'I' only applies to mental states.[6] In fact, there is no more room for the question, 'Am *I* the person eating this lunch?' than for a similar question about whether it is me who is having a particular thought. But this illusion of a particular adhesiveness between 'I' and mental states creates the picture of the ego as a persisting *mental* thing.

[5] Ludwig Wittgenstein: *The Blue Book*, in *The Blue and Brown Books*, Oxford, 1958, page 69.
[6] Gareth Evans: *The Varieties of Reference*, Oxford, 1982, pages 218–219.

Our life history

We naturally think of our life history as having a clear point when it begins, another clear point when it ends, and a certain kind of continuity between those points.

This way of thinking of the start of our life is found on both sides of the debate over abortion. There is a strong pull towards some clear line (at conception, at birth, or at some identifiable point somewhere between) where 'I' began.

Because the developmental process is more like an upward curve than a series of sharp jumps, thoughtful people may be unsure that the line they favour is defensible. But it is still natural to think of the matter in a way that is like the religious question of when the soul enters the body. We tend to think in terms of an instant when, like a light being turned on, I entered my body. The abortion issue is then argued in terms of who is most likely to have guessed the right moment.

We tend to think of death in the same way. At a certain moment, I depart, leaving behind a corpse. On some religious views, I am a soul that departs for an afterlife. In a secular version, I am something which at that point ceases to exist.

The belief in death and birth as sharp boundaries does not go well with the thought that I am identical with any particular set of my physical or mental characteristics. For they may emerge or fade away gradually. So this line of thought makes it again natural to think that I am not reducible to such features, but am an ego that owns them.

This is reinforced by an aspect of the psychology of ageing. People who are old sometimes say that 'in themselves' they do not feel any different from when they were young. We become directly aware of some features of our own ageing, such as forgetfulness and slowing up, but, apart from mirrors and the responses of other people, we might not realize that we are becoming grey and lined. These changes can seem somehow external, and can come as a shock when we notice them. The thought that the real me stays the same is easier to defend if the real me is not identified with my physical or mental features. They are too fugitive for the role.

Hegel's suggestion

=

It is not only when aware of ageing that we are reluctant to identify with our body. In his autobiography, Jean-Paul Sartre describes how he was considered a 'delicate' child, and felt that he and his body did not get on well: 'I confused my body with its sickness: I no longer knew which of the two was undesirable.'[7]

In case of illness, injury or handicap, it is natural for people to feel that *they* are not cramped or limited as their bodies are. And this thought can arise in those who have no sickness or impairment. Hegel believed that we each want as far as possible to be independent of the rest of the world. We see that our body depends for its life on things external to it. So, Hegel thought, we are tempted to withdraw the boundaries of the self. We exclude the body, and see ourselves as purely spiritual beings.

Hegel says that this gives an illusory picture of ourselves: the independence is illusory, because our awareness of ourselves depends on our bodies. To be self-conscious requires awareness of a contrast between myself and other things, and this depends on using our bodily sense organs. As Hegel puts it:

But in point of fact self-consciousness is the reflection out of the being of the world of sense and perception, and is essentially the return from *otherness*. As self-consciousness, it is movement; but since what it distinguishes from itself is *only itself as* itself, the difference, as an otherness, is *immediately superseded* for it; the difference *is not*, and *it* is only the motionless tautology of 'I am I'; but since for it the difference does not have the form of *being*, it is *not* self-consciousness.[8]

(Any reader of Hegel must feel some sympathy for the response of William James: 'The whole lesson of Kantian and post-Kantian speculation is, it seems to me, the lesson of simplicity. With Kant, complication both of thought and statement was an inborn infirmity, enhanced by the musty academicism of his Königsberg existence. With Hegel it was a raging fever. Terribly, therefore, do the sour grapes which these fathers of philosophy have eaten set our teeth on edge.'[9])

[7] Jean-Paul Sartre: *Words*, translated by Irene Clephane, Harmondsworth, 1967, page 57.
[8] G. W. F. Hegel: *Phenomenology of Spirit*, translated by A. V. Miller, Oxford, 1977, section 167.
[9] Op. cit., pages 365–366.

Apart from the cumbersomeness, it is hard to know how to respond to Hegel's idea. The supposed belief that, by thinking of myself as a purely spiritual being, I can escape from my physical dependence on the external world for such things as food and shelter, is absurd. Few people can literally have thought this. Such a belief might exist as a symptom of a type of pathological case. And pathological cases sometimes caricature milder tendencies within the normal range. So, it may be that many people who do not hold the belief consciously have some inclination towards it, or may even 'believe' it unconsciously. But, even on this rather generous interpretation, it is hard to see the Hegelian account as giving more than a small part of the explanation of the widespread inclination to believe in the ego.

Subjectivity

There is, as we have seen, a plausible case to be made for a more moderate version of the view that people transcend their bodies. This moderate version says that there is more to our experiences than can be specified by any description of them in physical or in functional terms.

It is still disputed how serious a problem our subjectivity is for functionalism. But it is easy to see how such thoughts can lead people towards belief in the ego. The view that I am more than my physical or functional properties looks like a premise of an argument for the ego. But it is worth saying that it is at best a premise. It does not on its own demonstrate that I am a Cartesian ego. If functionalism leaves out the subjective nature of experience, this shows that *one* reductionist account of mental states is inadequate. It does not show that we have to go back to a dualist view of the mind because *any* such attempt must fail. And, even if it did, a proof that mental states are non-physical would be no proof that they in turn must be owned by an ego.

The considerations mentioned so far, about language, our views about the start and end of life, and our inclination to think that there is more to us than can be described in physical or functional terms, are all very general. It is time to turn to the more specific features of our experience that make the Cartesian ego a natural belief.

Perception
==

When we perceive things, our experience depends on the causal mechanisms of our sensory systems. Knowing this inclines us to think of perception in terms of a partly misleading model that resembles cable television. This treats the neural links of the visual system as cable linking the outside world to an inner screen. The auditory system is a cable bringing sound. And the other sensory systems, although going beyond present television technology, are thought of on the same lines.

Our senses sometimes give us misleading information, in ways ranging from minor illusions to hallucinations. On the television model, the picture on the inner screen is subject to interference, or the soundtrack is distorted. The model also suggests the possibility of the picture on my screen being consistently distorted in ways I do not realize: perhaps the colours in your picture are not the same as those in mine. (Watching television, we think we see the colours as they are in front of the camera. But there is the experience of going to a shop selling televisions, and seeing them simultaneously giving their different versions of the colours.)

This model has its problems. How literally should it be taken? Can we ask questions about the size of the screen? Where is the screen? And, above all, who looks at the inner screen? These problems stop most people from literal belief in the model, but many of us are still half-consciously influenced by it.

To the extent that we think of seeing in terms of the inner screen, we are likely to have some blurred idea of the I who is looking at the screen. The model is sometimes ridiculed as 'the little man inside the head'. But we do not readily think of the screen being watched by a little man who himself has eyes. The infinite regress raised by *his* visual system looms too close. The screen tends to be non-physical. The model is then sketchily completed with the screen being looked at by me: a disembodied observer, or Cartesian ego.

Although the ego is thought of as disembodied, it is also, perhaps inconsistently, thought of as being located. I am a couple of inches behind the eyes. This fits with the central role of the brain, but was a natural way of thinking before we knew what the brain does, as it is the point of view from which we see the world. If the eyes had been situated in the stomach or the small of the back, we might have had different intuitive ideas about the location of the self.

Decision and action
===

Our experience of action can also generate belief in the ego. One way of thinking of the body is as a vehicle we use to get about in. Spraining an ankle frustrates my plans in rather the way a flat tyre does. These thoughts can generate a picture in which I occupy my body as a driver occupies a car. The centre of decision and control that is me can either be thought of as a functional system in the brain, or as the disembodied ego.

The experience of taking decisions also influences us here. We sometimes want to do incompatible things and decide to act on one desire rather than another. It does not always feel as if this is just a matter of the stronger desire elbowing the weaker one aside. It can feel more as if I am like a judge, not identified with either side, but calmly weighing up both cases before coming down on one side. This suggests that I have a role in decision that is to some extent independent of the desires involved.

The strongest expression of this view of decisions is in Kant's theory of the 'rational will'. In the Kantian account of our psychology, actions are not autonomous when controlled by desires. Freedom only exists when the will takes a decision based on reason alone, independent of any desire. The picture is of desires pulling in different directions, like members of a committee voting in different ways. Then the will takes the decision, like someone in the chair using the casting vote. Kant's will, able to override any set of desires, is like someone able to use the chair's casting vote to overrule even a large majority of the committee.

This picture of the will's decisions being free of the influence of desires has been much criticized. It seems obscure and implausible. What is the will, and how does it operate? What is it to be motivated by reason alone? How can I have a reason to act which is in no way connected with anything I want? No explanation is given of how the decision is either reached or implemented. But, whatever the weaknesses of this model, it grows out of a natural picture of ourselves adjudicating between desires. And the rational will, in its detachment, is the ego applied to action.

Has the ego a role?

===

Some of the reasons that may influence us to believe in the ego do not stand up to scrutiny. We do not have to assume that there must be some thing which a pronoun refers to. And, because I am detachable from some of my properties, it does not follow that I am detachable from all of them. (There are knives that have lost their blades, and knives that have lost their handles, but no knives that have lost both.) If we are influenced by the hope Hegel detected, of escaping dependence on the physical world, that does not stand up to scrutiny either. And even if the subjectivity of experience eludes functionalism, this takes us only part of the way to belief in the ego. The models of perception and action which tacitly invoke the ego are more influential than convincing.

The remaining part of the case for the ego is its role in giving unity to a person. The idea comes from my experience not being fragmented. I am not only seeing, but also hearing, tasting, and so on. And I am conscious of these experiences simultaneously. My experience is united in the way that of a split brain patient perhaps is not. Particularly when combined with the model of the inner screen, the inner soundtrack, and so on, this can make the ego seem plausible. It could be thought that the unity of experience is explained by the fact that a single ego is aware of it all at the same time. In the same way it could be said that the unity of someone's life is explained by its being lived and experienced by an ego that lasts the whole lifetime. We have seen that neural links may be a more satisfactory explanation of the unity of consciousness at a particular time. And perhaps the persistence of an integrated brain better explains the unity of a person over a lifetime. There is a lot we do not yet know about the brain, but compared to its potential explanatory power, that of the metaphysical ego looks dim.

It is natural for people to think of themselves in terms of an ego that gives unity to their experiences and their lives. But the case for this natural conception is shaky. It is reasonable to hope for a more impressive alternative.

CHAPTER TEN

═══

ALTERNATIVES
TO THE EGO

Is the truth depressing? Some may find it so. But I find it liberating, and consoling. When I believed that my existence was such a further fact, I seemed imprisoned in myself. My life seemed like a glass tunnel, through which I was moving faster every year, and at the end of which there was darkness. When I changed my view, the walls of my glass tunnel disappeared. I now live in the open air.

DEREK PARFIT: *Reasons and Persons.*

THE CASE FOR believing in the ego is made up of a number of different strands. Each strand, considered separately, is rather unimpressive. We cannot observe the ego, and it has little or no explanatory power. We have sufficient reason to abandon it. The discussion now moves on to alternatives to the ego, and their implications.

We are not naturally impartial between ourselves and others. We take a quite special interest in what happens to us. I read the figures for early deaths from cancer or heart disease and hope that I will not become one of them. Thoughts of this kind do not seem to depend on answering problems about what exactly 'I' refers to.

Whether it is my body, my brain, or my mental history which is essential to my identity does not matter much in everyday life. The different views about personal identity normally converge. My brain is not separated from my body. My hemispheres are not each linked by radio with half of someone else's brain. I do not have multiple personality. My physical and mental life flows along as a single stream. If an accident gives me amnesia, or I develop senile dementia, or my corpus callosum is severed, there may be a problem, but otherwise the questions seem academic. Belief in the ego may be natural to us, but giving it up does not seem likely to change our lives.

This reassuring view has recently been challenged, and looks a good deal less secure than it did. The challenge has come from Derek Parfit's exploration of the implications of giving up belief in the ego.[1]

The partial convergence of the bodily and mental approaches

If we eliminate the ego, which was supposed to 'own' my physical and mental characteristics and their joint history, we are left simply with those characteristics and their history. The question then is which characteristics are essential. Are there any features whose destruction would be the end of *me*?

Because these features come together in ordinary life, philosophers have used thought experiments to prize them apart. In particular, they have tried to separate physical from psychological continuity. 'Reincarnation' cases have been imagined, in which someone turns up claiming, with apparently good evidence, to remember being some long dead historical character. Or a technology of 'brain wiping' has been envisaged: a brain is wiped clean of someone's memories, attitudes, beliefs, intentions and so on, and then reprogrammed with those of someone else. Your brain and mine are each wiped and then reprogrammed with the material from each other's. Different theories of personal identity give different answers to the question of which, if either, of the resulting people I will be.[2]

A striking feature of the discussion of such cases has been the tendency of physical and psychological approaches to move towards each other. We have seen how, in the context of an approach emphasizing the body, the importance of my mental life suggests the preeminence of the brain. And we have also seen how dubiously intelligible is the idea of free-floating experiences. An experience has to be 'localized' in one system of consciousness or another. And it is hard to see how this could be done except by reference to a body or brain.

[1] Derek Parfit: *Reasons and Persons*, Oxford, 1984.
[2] Sydney Shoemaker: *Self-Knowledge and Self-Identity*, Ithaca, 1963; Bernard Williams: *Problems of the Self*, Cambridge, 1973, chapters 1 and 4.

But the convergence is not total. In the brain wipe case, a bodily theorist who accepts the special role of the brain may say that I am where my original brain is. And a psychological theorist, who accepts the role of the body or brain in identifying streams of consciousness, may disagree. On this view, although *my* stream of consciousness is identified by its origins in my brain, there is enough continuity to show that it has now moved to the other brain. And, on this view, that shows that *I* have moved there.

In computer terms, the residual disagreement is over whether I am the hardware of a particular brain or the software with which it is programmed. (No doubt the brain cannot really have its programme changed like a computer. This is a thought experiment, not a discussion of likely developments in neurology.)

It is hard to see how to resolve this disagreement. We may even start to wonder what it is about. If we believed in the ego, it would still be hard to settle the issue, but at least we would know (at one level) what we were discussing: whether the ego was still over here 'in' this brain or had gone over there to that one. The debate would be like the old version of the abortion debate, conducted in terms of whether the soul had yet entered the foetus.

If I know that you and I are both going to be given brain wipes, and reprogrammed with material from each other's brain, I may wonder which of the resulting people will be me. Perhaps, as in a case invented by Bernard Williams, one of them will be given a lot of money and the other will be tortured, and I have some say in who gets which.[3] Selfishly, I hope it will be me who will get the money rather than be tortured. But, at first sight, it seems possible that my efforts towards this can be based on a mistake. Suppose I arrange for one of them to get the money, in the belief that he will be me, but it turns out that the other one is *really* me?

But what is the possibility of mistake here? If there is not an ego whose location we can be wrong about, what mistake can there be? After the brain wipe, there are two people. One is partly continuous with you and partly continuous with me. So is the other, though the continuities are reversed. We may wonder whether there is any further fact about who either of them really is. Perhaps thinking that way is a residue of the ego, which (although not physical) was thought of as located in one place or another.

[3] Op. cit., chapter 4.

Closest continuers
==

One move away from such thinking has been made by Robert Nozick.[4] He suggests that what counts as me is the best of the available candidates. This is the one he calls the 'closest continuer', or the one in which the most, or the most important, of my features are found. On this view, being me is a relative affair. Being me can be like being king. There can be someone who would have been me, had there not been a more direct descendant with a stronger claim. But, as with being king, there is no half-way stage. You either are or are not the king. And, on Nozick's view, any future person either will or will not be me. This fits with the all-or-none logic of identity statements. If A is identical with B and B is identical with C, then A is identical with C. There is no room for the identity relation somehow fading out between A and C.

Nozick's relativizing move is a decisive break from ways of thought still influenced by the model of the ego. It gets away from the idea that being me is some kind of absolute metaphysical fact. But there are reasons for wondering whether it goes far enough.

From identity to survival: Parfit
==

Parfit's discussion opens with another thought experiment: the Teletransporter. To travel, you go into a cubicle, where a scanner destroys your body, but transmits every detail of it to a replicator, where an identical version of it (including the brain, programmed with the same memories and mental life) is reproduced. On one account, you have travelled to the other end. On another account, you have been killed and only a replica of you created.

The issue seems to be whether the replica is me: a question about identity. But the thrust of Parfit's argument is that such identity questions may not have a determinate answer, and that they are less important than we think. He argues that what matters is not identity, but survival. Travelling to New York by Teletransporter may not

[4] Robert Nozick: *Philosophical Explanations*, Oxford, 1981, chapter 1.

preserve my identity in the way going by Concorde does, but it gives a kind of survival that is virtually as good. The mental life of the replica is connected with my present mental life in the ways that matter: he will carry out my plans, be influenced by memories of my past life, and so on. Survival is a matter of preserving such psychological links. And this kind of survival, rather than identity, is what really matters in ordinary life too.

The logic of identity is all-or-none. But survival is a matter of degree. If these psychological links are what matter to us, the logic of identity is too Procrustean for our concerns. In some of the science fiction cases, I can survive partly in one of the resulting people, and partly in another. (In denying this, the closest continuer view retains a Procrustean residue from belief in the ego.)

And, in the real world, multiple personality and the split brain cases can be interpreted along similar lines. If a particular case of multiple personality is better interpreted as two people than as one, there may still not be the complete gap that there is between you and me. Each personality may contain partial residues of the other. And, if the split brain patients are best interpreted as two people, a similar qualification holds. The unified person before the operation partly survives in each of the two resulting people. Their separateness is qualified, not only by their sharing a body, but also by their sharing a history.

The idea of degrees of survival does not in the real world apply only to bizarre pathology. I can expect only partial survival over a long stretch of my life. The psychological unity of a life is not all-or-none. Memories or intentions can fade or disappear. I can be linked psychologically to other stages of my life to a greater or lesser degree. If I am hit in old age by senile dementia, perhaps nearly all my present self will have faded out. And perhaps there is very little of my five-year-old self left in me now. (George Orwell saw this fading in people, saw it was similar to what happens in nations, but thought that in both cases identity persisted: 'What can the England of 1940 have in common with the England of 1840? But then, what have you in common with the child of five whose photograph your mother keeps on the mantelpiece? Nothing, except that you happen to be the same person.') [5]

Once we abandon the ego, it is hard to resist Parfit's conclusions.

[5] George Orwell: *The Lion and the Unicorn*, Harmondsworth, 1982, page 37.

This is because we are left only with our empirical characteristics, both physical and psychological. And these can be altered gradually. If we stick to the all-or-none logic of identity, we will have to say, at some point along a series of incremental changes, that one more slight change (such as the loss of one more memory) will be the end of *me*. Our worry about such changes seems better reflected by thinking in terms of degrees of survival.

Some possible consequences

The consequences Parfit sees as following from this are radical. The unity of a person across a lifetime seems to him, not only a matter of degree, but also something less important or deep than has been thought. He talks in terms of earlier and later selves existing at different stages of a single lifetime. (Though by this he does not mean there are sharp boundaries between different selves: his comparison is with different historical periods in a nation's history.) An earlier self does not abruptly stop, but fades, so that little of it may be left at a later stage.

This view has possible consequences for desert. Do I deserve to pay a penalty (or to be rewarded) for something I did many years ago? Desert is not totally eliminated. But its importance is much reduced if we accept that the person who did the act was not my present self, but a past self who has almost completely faded out. There are similar possible conclusions about commitments. Should I keep a promise I made to you years ago? Or is the commitment weaker if I can argue that the promise was made, not by me to you, but by my past self to your past self? On this view, both desert and commitments seem as fugitive as our past selves.

This may suggest that the demands of morality are weakened by thinking in terms of degrees of survival. But, in another way they could be increased. If I take up smoking, putting present pleasure before future health, I am open to some kind of criticism. Conventionally, this is that I am being foolish, doing what is against my interests. But, if this is seen as a present self harming a future self, the criticism may be that it is immoral: harming not me but some later person. Apparently 'paternalistic' intervention to stop someone smoking might be easier to justify: it would be a case of stopping one person from harming another.

Parfit also believes his view can lessen the fear of death. After his death, there will still be experiences influenced by his present experiences. People will have memories of his life, or will have thoughts influenced by him:

My death will break the more direct relations between my present experiences and future experiences, but it will not break various other relations. This is all there is to the fact that there will be no one living who will be me. Now that I have seen this, my death seems to me less bad.

Instead of saying, 'I shall be dead', I should say, 'There will be no future experiences that will be related, in certain ways, to these present experiences'. Because it reminds me what this fact involves, this redescription makes this fact less depressing.[6]

The separateness of persons

These thoughts about death are linked with Parfit's downplaying of the importance of the separateness of different people.

Utilitarianism tells us to aim for the greatest general happiness, and this sometimes involves sacrificing the interests of some people to those of others. People who find this unacceptable have a diagnosis of why utilitarianism goes wrong. John Rawls has suggested that it does so because it allows no real place for the separateness of persons.[7] People are separate in a way that makes it unacceptable to justify a harm to you by citing a greater benefit to me. Within my own life I can justify a present sacrifice by a future benefit, but we should not add up gains and losses across different lives, as though *who* gains or loses makes no difference. It is as if utilitarians treat different people as part of one super-person.

Parfit sees the move from identity to survival as having implications that greatly weaken the force of this appeal to distributive justice. To think in terms of degrees of survival raises the possibility of distributive justice between earlier and later selves. He says that utilitarianism 'may be supported by, not the conflation of persons,

6 Parfit: op. cit., page 281.
7 John Rawls: *A Theory of Justice*, Cambridge, Mass., 1971, sections 5 and 30.

but their partial disintegration. It may rest upon the view that a person's life is less deeply integrated than most of us assume'. He says that the implicit utilitarian belief that it makes no moral difference where benefits and burdens come 'may be partly supported by the view that the unity of each life, and hence the difference between lives, is in its nature less deep'.[8]

If Parfit's claims are right, the abandonment of the ego is not some little upheaval in academic philosophy. On his view, it changes the way we think of our future lives and our death. It alters the boundaries of justifiable intervention in the lives of others, and changes the way we see our commitments to them. It undermines a common foundation for belief in distributive justice and in individual rights. It is this last feature which has sometimes caused particular shock. One reviewer of Parfit's book said that, if this is the new wave in moral philosophy, we had better start building breakwaters.[9]

Some comments

Without the ego, it is plausible that it is survival rather than identity that matters. And the psychological links that constitute survival hold to varying degrees. Parfit's brilliant development of this case is widely and rightly held to be one of the finest pieces of work in contemporary philosophy.

But some of the conclusions seem to me unconvincing. I do not find the proposed way of thinking of death particularly consoling. And I am sceptical about the views on commitments and on the reduced importance of the separateness of persons.

The views on all three topics are linked to the view that 'a person's life is less deeply integrated than most of us assume'. If my own life is not as integrated as I had thought, it may matter less that, after my death, various experiences will turn up in someone else's life rather than mine. And, if both of us have less integrated lives, then perhaps it was only our past selves who made promises to each other. And, as integration is reduced, the boundaries between us may become hardly more important than the boundaries between our earlier and later selves.

[8] Parfit: op. cit., page 336.
[9] Shirley Robin Lettwin, *The Spectator*, 1984.

But this idea that we are not so deeply integrated as we assume does not simply follow from the abandonment of the ego. Take the nation analogy. Perhaps there have been patriots who believed that their country had a metaphysical 'soul'. Disillusion with the metaphysics would have a weakening effect to the extent that their patriotism depended on the national soul. But there are patriots who have no such beliefs. And their belief that their country is deeply integrated may be true. (Some countries are and some are not.) Metaphysics is not the only basis for integration.

The case for weakened integration (or the case against it) needs a fuller picture of our psychology than is presented. Here the contrast in philosophy analogous to that between abstract and representational art is relevant. The case against the ego is well suited to the abstract style, with highly theoretical considerations developed by science fiction examples. But these techniques may not suit the question of how integrated the lives of actual people are. Something more like representational art may be needed. The abstract style leads to a highly schematic psychology, which may underrate both the unity of a single life and the resulting significance of the boundaries between lives.

Giving up belief in the ego leaves us with nothing more than our physical and psychological features. These may be fast fading compared to the permanence of a metaphysical ego. But it is an empirical question how stable or fugitive they are. It is also possible that a coherent pattern sometimes underlies some of the visible changes. Without the ego, the episodes of a life can seem like a heap of stones. Then perhaps death is less important. It does not much matter whether some extra stones are dumped on my pile or on some other one. But, if I see the stones as part of a building I am creating, being cut off with too few stones can ruin everything.

I am inclined towards this more architectural view. I agree that we should move from valuing identity to survival. But if we treat survival as something that matters in itself, it may be hard to see it as very important. Perhaps our concern for survival is not just a matter of caring that certain kinds of experiences should exist. (If it were, it might be hard to see why it should matter in whose life they occurred.) Perhaps survival is itself only of instrumental value. For some of us, our interest in it may partly derive from our hopes of what we can make of our lives. These hopes are the topic of the rest of the book.

PART TWO

===

SELF-CREATION

═══

CHAPTER ELEVEN

FOLK PSYCHOLOGY

The men of experiment are like the ant; they only collect and use. The reasoners resemble spiders, who make cob-webs out of their own substance. But the bee takes a middle course; it gathers its material from the flowers of the garden and of the field, but transforms and digests it by a power of its own. Not unlike this is the true business of philosophy.

FRANCIS BACON: *First Book of Aphorisms.*

WE HAVE SEEN that people are more fragmented, or at least more of a federation, than we usually think. But we have also looked at factors underlying the unity of the federation: the self-consciousness of a single person. We care a lot about being a person, and look with horror on anything, whether death or some neurological catastrophe, that threatens to obliterate this self-consciousness.

In normal life, outside neurological or psychiatric disorders, and with brain transplants and Teletransporters not yet here, we do not worry about whether we are identical with some previous person, or ask, of several future people, 'Which one will be me?' And in normal life we do not have to worry about where the frontier comes between us and the world. The Martian scientist's perspective was introduced to reduce the sense of obviousness, to dramatize conditions of self-consciousness we might otherwise not notice. These conditions of self-consciousness are normally so massively satisfied that we have to use imagination to see how things might have been different.

Yet, in normal life, people do ask questions about their own identity. And the answers matter to them in a way the science fiction problems do not. In asking these questions, they are using the word 'identity' in a way philosophers usually do not. They are not asking where they stop and the rest of the world begins, or which of several people they are. Rather, they are thinking about what they are like: about the characteristics that make them distinctive, the things that make friendship with them different from friendship with someone else.

I shall make several claims here. The main one is that our individuality is not something just given to us, but is, in part, something we ourselves create. The way we think of ourselves, and of our past, has a special role in this self-creation. Other things in the world, and other people, are not changed directly by the way we think of them. But our conception of ourselves does directly influence what we are like. I shall argue that, contrary to a common belief, a scientific view of people is compatible with our shaping our own characteristics. And I shall suggest that shaping ourselves is a more important aspect of us than is usually supposed. It should be given a central place in our thinking about social and political issues.

Psychology and common sense
==

The case for some of these claims is inevitably psychological. Part of the problem in making such a case is the fragmented state of psychology.

On the one hand there are large systems, like Freud's and others in the psychoanalytic tradition, which give an overall framework for thinking about people. A problem with these systems is that they seem free-floating: their links with evidence are hard to pin down. To read a book in this tradition is often to be confronted with claims that seem authoritative. These claims are apparently based on a body of knowledge, but you never seem to be reading the book where the supporting evidence is given.

On the other hand there is the more experimental approach to psychology. This has transformed our understanding of such topics as perception. The same approach, together with the development of artificial intelligence, is starting to transform our understanding of thought and language. But this experimental approach has so far not helped us so much with the more personal aspects of ourselves: with motivation, relationships and our emotional life. In these more elusive fields, the experimental approach has not been useless. Facts have been produced, sometimes striking ones, but they form a miscellaneous heap, waiting for some explanatory theory to organize them. It can sometimes seem to psychologists that they are waiting for a Newton to produce the underlying principles.

But psychologists do use a framework of theory. They use the 'common-sense' explanations used by detectives, novelists, historians, juries, and by all of us when thinking about our friends. (Or rather, they use these as their overall theory, except when some approach such as behaviourism leads them to replace the ordinary framework with something cruder.) This common-sense framework explains what people do in terms of what they believe, what they want, what they hope for and are afraid of, their moods, what they like, who they love or hate, their ambition, their jealousy, their embarrassment, and so on.

The centre of this common-sense psychology is the belief-desire model of action. When people do things, the standard explanation cites some combination of their beliefs and desires. Chamberlain signed the Munich agreement because he wanted peace and he believed Hitler could be trusted. Your uncle gave you a green china frog for Christmas because he wanted to please you and he believed you would like it. Using beliefs and desires to explain action is the core of common-sense psychology. But the belief-desire model interacts with a broader set of common-sense explanations, citing other factors, such as moods. It was because he was in that enthusiastic mood that he thought you would like the china frog.

These common-sense explanations are so familiar and so intuitively obvious that we do not think of them as constituting a theoretical framework. But they do. And not seeing this is a pity, because when a theory is not recognized it is often left hazy and unexamined. Unsatisfactory parts get removed or changed only when we see that this *is* our explanatory theory, and so start to take seriously how well it works.

If experimental psychologists largely ignore the everyday explanatory framework, the same cannot be said of philosophers. In the dominant tradition in philosophy of mind, the common-sense concepts, and the explanation of action in terms of belief and desire, are subjected to increasing refinement. But, with some notable exceptions, there is not much thought about whether it needs changing. Some philosophical approaches fit the description Tolstoy gives, in his *Confession*, of 'professional philosophy, which serves only to divide all existing phenomena into new philosophical columns with new names'.[1]

There are plenty of psychological ants and philosophical spiders, but not many bees.

Some philosophers have reacted against the dominant approach. They have argued that common-sense psychology, particularly the belief–desire model of action, is a pre-scientific theory, which should be abandoned in favour of something better based. They have attacked it as 'folk psychology', a set of supposed explanations of dubious power. Paul Churchland has said of folk psychology that it

... suffers explanatory failures on an epic scale, that it has been stagnant for at least twenty-five centuries, and that its categories appear (so far) to be incommensurable with or orthogonal to the categories of the background physical science whose long-term claim to explain human behaviour seems undeniable. Any theory that meets this description must be allowed a serious candidate for outright elimination.[2]

Opponents of folk psychology do not always attack the whole network of everyday psychological explanations. It is more common to give a narrower account of the folk psychology to be eliminated. On this view, we should stop citing 'propositional attitudes', such as beliefs and desires, as causes of what people do. One problem with this is that there seems to be no alternative explanatory model of remotely the same scope and power. Perhaps one could be developed, though it is hard even to imagine what it would be like. But certainly it is not now available.

To abandon beliefs and desires as explanations of actions, we would need an explanatory model that was both an alternative and an improvement. This sets the standard rather high, as our present scheme has evolved to accommodate a great deal of knowledge of people. It has been suggested that evolutionary pressures have favoured our becoming naturally good psychologists, able to imagine others from the inside, and so predict what they will do.[3]

Whatever the merits of the evolutionary explanation, social life is

---

[1] Leo Tolstoy: *Confession*, translated by David Patterson, New York, 1983, page 43.
[2] P. M. Churchland: Eliminative Materialism and Propositional Attitudes, *Journal of Philosophy*, 1981.
[3] Nicholas Humphrey: *Consciousness Regained*, London, 1983.

clearly based on the fact that a lot of the time we understand each other rather well. And this perceptiveness has sometimes reached an extraordinary level of subtlety. (P. F. Strawson, talking of the attack on folk psychology, refers to 'the terms employed by such simple folk as Shakespeare, Tolstoy, Proust, and Henry James'.) [4]

It would be dogmatic to say that we will never find a better model for explaining actions. But our present model has some life in it still, and it seems worth continuing to develop it as new evidence comes in. (Though one problem is that it is not clear what the boundaries of 'folk psychology' are, and so the line between revision and abandonment is blurred.)

Some possibilities of progress in folk psychology

Progress in psychological explanation comes with new evidence. But it also comes with greater precision and clarity in our models and concepts, so that the possibility of a conflict with evidence is sharpened.

These processes go together. Take our understanding of the emotions. We start with our present rather vague concepts of different emotions. We try to correlate emotions with chemical states in the brain. But this leads us to discover chemical systems, based on different neurotransmitters. And we start to see an alternative way of classifying the emotions.

Our present classification is partly based on the objects of emotions: the threat we fear, or the rudeness we are annoyed about. It is partly based on the contexts in which emotions arise, on the behaviour associated with them, and on their characteristic 'feel'. Wittgenstein wrote disparagingly of 'the classifications of philosophers and psychologists: they classify clouds by their shape'.[5] To work out the different chemical pathways is to move towards a classification with more power to explain our emotional clouds.

This is not to belittle the understanding of the emotions shown by Shakespeare, Tolstoy, Proust, and Henry James. To know the

[4] P. F. Strawson: *Scepticism and Naturalism, Some Varieties*, Oxford, 1984.
[5] Ludwig Wittgenstein: *Zettel*, edited by G.E.M. Anscombe and G.H. von Wright, translated by G.E.M. Anscombe, Oxford, 1967, section 462.

underlying chemical structures is a supplement, rather than an alternative, to understanding our emotional life from the inside. And the development of the chemically based classification allows us to raise new questions about the relations between love, anxiety, hatred, jealousy, fear and other 'traditional' emotions. Perhaps anger turns off sexual arousal because some chemicals inhibit the action of others. There may be far more subtle psychological connections of this sort, to be discovered when we can read back from the chemistry to the psychology.

It may be felt that this extension of understanding of the emotions is more like an alternative to folk psychology than a development of it. So let us take a different area where there is hope of progress without going down to the physiological or chemical level of explanation.

A lot of our understanding of people is intuitive: it does not depend on any conscious process of interpreting evidence. And we are often quite unable to say exactly what it is based on. Ted Hughes describes the way we form first impressions of people:

Usually, from our first meeting with a person, we get some single main impression, of like or dislike, confidence or distrust, reality or artificiality, or some single, vivid something that we cannot pin down in more than a tentative, vague phrase. That little phrase is like the visible moving fin of a great fish in a dark pool: we can see only the fin: we cannot see the fish, let alone catch or lift it out. Or usually we cannot. Sometimes we can. And some people have a regular gift for it.[6]

These impressions of people, and our beliefs about what they are like, are not the result of telepathy. They must be based on unconscious processes of inference and classification. These processes are what parodists exploit. It is hard to *say* which features of Hitler were captured by Charlie Chaplin, but we see the parody at once. It must be possible to work out the way in which subliminally noticed aspects of someone's gestures, tone of voice, facial expression, or style of dress, can feed into a typology of people, which is in turn linked both to the beliefs about character and to responses of our own. Our beliefs about people, and the boxes in which we fit each other, are things we have only started to explore.

There is a parallel with our recognition of faces. Someone may

[6] Ted Hughes: *Poetry in the Making*, London, 1967, page 121.

have a face a bit like General de Gaulle. That is how we have to describe it, as we have hardly any names for kinds of faces, despite our massive capacity to recognize them, and despite our having a special area of the brain for doing so. Our understanding of recognition will grow when we start to work out our unconscious typology.

There is a similar typology of beliefs waiting to be worked out. Often, talking to someone about one issue, it is possible to make an informed guess about their views about other, logically unrelated, matters. I know Mrs Mary Whitehouse only as a campaigner against pornography, but I would expect to be right more often than by chance if I tried to predict her views on euthanasia, strikes, embryo research, nuclear disarmament, and the importance of tidiness in the home.

There are here two possible fields of investigation. One is the mapping out of these different styles of thinking and patterns of belief, together with explaining how they arise. The other comes from the thought that my prediction about Mrs Whitehouse may be altogether too confident. If she challenged me to make my predictions, she could well turn out to be splendidly unpredictable (at least by me). But, if so, there is still a field to investigate: my beliefs about her beliefs. For, whether or not we are correct, we do have these beliefs about beliefs. We ascribe beliefs to others in clusters, often going well beyond any evidence we could explicitly cite.

Critics of folk psychology have seen the concept of belief as a prime candidate for being given up. Stephen Stich has developed a powerful case for the view that the unitary concept of belief may need to be replaced by a set of different concepts, each more fine-grained than our present one.[7] Perhaps this case will prevail. But, if so, it is hard to accept that all that we now think we know about beliefs will be seen as utter rubbish. It seems more likely that the great bulk of what we now believe about belief will survive translation into the new, more sophisticated concepts. And if part of psychological progress is to understand how we think about the world, and how we think about other people, questions about beliefs (and about beliefs about beliefs) seem some of the most promising we could investigate.

[7] Stephen Stich: *From Folk Psychology to Cognitive Science, The Case Against Belief*, Cambridge, Mass., 1983.

Towards a folk psychology of personal identity

===

The following chapters attempt to sketch out a piece of one version of our folk psychology: the part concerning our sense of what we are like, and about the role of our own decisions in influencing this. The aim is not just to describe what people believe, but to reconstruct a version that can be defended as likely to be true.

However, the aim is not to produce a scientifically established account of these matters. That, if it is possible at all, would require much more supporting evidence than I can provide. Rather, the strategy is to cite some of the phenomena which our framework of thought must accommodate, and to sketch out a way in which it might do so.

In trying to cite cases which our thinking has to account for, I shall not normally quote results of properly controlled experimental studies. I shall more often quote accounts of what people have done, or else things people have said or written about themselves. At times, use will be made of imaginary cases, and of novels.

The unscientific nature of all this will be obvious. The reader should approach these pieces of evidence with the sceptical approach of a historian. The questions to ask are: 'Does what is being said sound plausible? Does it fit with what other people have said about similar things? Does it fit with my experience of my own life, or my experience of what people are like? Does the account have the ring of truth, or does the tone of voice suggest an unreliable witness? And, if the account is true, can we extrapolate to what human beings are like in general, or does it just show something about a particular person, or about a particular group in a certain society at a certain time?'

This discussion attempts, on a smaller scale, to follow the model of such a project given by William James in his *Principles of Psychology*. In attempting this, I have been daunted by how well James carried it out. But I have also often been reminded of a severe remark made by Wittgenstein about Goethe's theory of the origin of the spectrum He said, 'it is really not a theory at all. *Nothing* can be predicted by means of it. It is, rather, a vague schematic outline, of the sort we find in James's psychology'.[8]

The approach James adopted does not lead to predictions of a scientifically reliable kind. Though this is not to say that it has absolutely no predictive value. If, after reading James, we have more understanding of people, this can feed into the predictions we make. When we get to know someone well, we may be better placed to anticipate the kind of thing they are likely to do, without feeling that we can predict them like clockwork.

In this kind of psychology there is always a risk of vagueness and platitude. But I hope we can do a bit better than this. We each have a set of background beliefs about what people are like. We know many facts about individual people, and we each have a picture, blurred in places, inexplicit and incomplete, of how these facts about people hang together. We each tend to take our own picture as *the* picture. The method here is to try to make one such account more explicit, trying to modify and shape it in the light of some evidence. Perhaps spelling out one such account will bring out points of disagreement with others. And, if so, we can then look for more evidence, and perhaps as a result make some progress in understanding what people are like.

[8] Ludwig Wittgenstein: *Remarks on Colour*, edited by G. E. M. Anscombe, translated by Linda McAlister and Margarete Schättle, Oxford, 1977, section 125.

CHAPTER TWELVE

═══

FREUD'S EGO

W E CONTRAST ourselves with the rest of the world. For this contrast, my frontier is the edge of my body. But I can also draw an internal frontier between myself and some of my physical or mental states. Yet these states are still mine: they do not belong to anyone else.

Among my physical states, I may regard bodily damage, or perhaps some natural feature, as alien to me. And in my mental life, I may distinguish between what I do and what happens to me independent of my conscious control. At times I deliberately direct my attention on to something, while at other times thoughts or images come unbidden to mind. And we sometimes feel ourselves to be struggling against psychological forces which are stronger than we are. But, if these things are all internal to me, how can I feel detached from them? What conception of myself am I using to draw this contrast? One of the most interesting sets of answers to these questions is Freud's account of this internal frontier.

A problem is raised for any discussion of Freud's ideas by their extreme holism. They form an elaborately interconnected system, giving an account of child development, of the origin and cure of neuroses, of our sex life, of dreams, of jokes and slips of the tongue, of crowd psychology, and of religion and war. When questions are raised about some particular aspect of Freud's ideas, the defence often seems to be that the theory as a whole has proved its explanatory power elsewhere. It is hard to disentangle the account, say, of dreams, to assess its truth independently of the whole system. For this reason, some people treat Freud's theories as a religion. Small modifications may be allowed, but the overall account is treated as beyond serious doubt. For the same reason, others discard the theories as unscientific speculation, about on a par with phrenology. These rival responses to Freud's holism combine to prevent scrutiny of his theories.

Here I hope to separate as far as possible Freud's account of the Ego from the rest of his theories. As a first approximation, it can be said that Freud called the centre of control in a person the 'I'. He contrasted the I with the It: the origin of involuntary thoughts, images and desires.

In talking of the I and the It rather than of the Ego and the Id, I am following Freud rather than his translators. He wrote of *das Ich und das Es*, using the German pronouns meaning 'I' and 'It'. His intention here was to develop, rather than abandon, the concepts of folk psychology. He defended his use of the everyday pronouns:

You will probably object to our having chosen simple pronouns to denote our two agencies or provinces of the soul, instead of giving them orotund Greek names. In psychoanalysis, however, we like to keep in contact with the popular mode of thinking and prefer to make its concepts scientifically serviceable rather than to reject them ... The impersonal 'it' is immediately connected with certain forms of expression used by normal people. 'It shot through me', people say; 'there was something in me at that moment that was stronger than me'.[1]

Bruno Bettelheim has pointed out how many associations we lose in moving from the subjective intimacy of 'I' to the impersonal 'Ego'.[2] We are more inclined to think of 'I' from inside, and, since the conscious, rational part of us is called the 'I', we are encouraged to side with it against the other parts of ourselves. The intuitive associations of 'it' noticed by Freud are similarly lacking for the 'Id'. Bettelheim has noted that *das Es* has even stronger associations in German. When young, all Germans are referred to by the neuter pronoun *es*, which gives Freud's term echoes of a time when they had less control over their irrational impulses. Although not all the associations of Freud's German come over in the English words, fewer are lost than if we adopt the orotund Latin names.

Freud's account of the I is partly developmental. It also combines an account of various mental functions with a speculative neurophysiology of their location in the brain. Because he does not

[1] *The Question of Lay Analysis*, translated by James Strachey, in *Two Short Accounts of Psychoanalysis*, Harmondsworth, 1962, page 105.
[2] Bruno Bettelheim: *Freud and Man's Soul*, London, 1983, pages 53–64.

clearly distinguish these strands, his functional account is often embedded in spatial terminology. Different elements of his theory were given prominence at different times. I will give a brief outline of his theory, treating the different accounts he gave as part of a unified view. The aim is not historical but analytical: to try to separate and examine the different components.

Freud's account in outline

Freud divides mental states and functions into those that are conscious, preconscious and unconscious. What is preconscious can be brought to consciousness at will: most of the time I am not thinking of my own name or of the the square root of forty-nine, but I can easily do so. Unconscious states are more deeply inaccessible: Freud thinks people have emotions and desires which are unlikely to surface without the help of psychoanalysis.

For Freud, the idea of consciousness as the surface of the mind is more than a metaphor. He thinks a person starts as an unconscious It, on whose surface is the perceptual system, which is the nucleus around which the conscious I forms. Here 'surface' is partly to be taken literally, as the part of the brain near the skull.

The It is 'the dark, inaccessible part of our personality'.[3] It is the part of the mind where logic does not rule, where contradictory impulses are found side by side. 'We call it a chaos, a cauldron full of seething excitations.'[4] The processes of the It are not governed by any awareness of time. 'The sole prevailing quality of the It is that of being unconscious.'[5]

On the surface of this dark inner region ('developed out of its cortical layer')[6] emerges the conscious and organized mental life of the I: the part of the It modified by perception of the external world. There is no sharp separation. The lower part of the I merges into the It. The most striking difference is the coherence of the I: 'What distinguishes the I from the It quite especially is a tendency to syn-

[3] *New Introductory Lectures on Psychoanalysis*, translated by James Strachey, London, 1933, Lecture 31.
[4] Ibid.
[5] *An Outline of Psychoanalysis*, translated by James Strachey, London, 1940, chapter 4.
[6] Ibid., chapter 8.

thesis in its contents, to a combination and unification in its mental processes that are totally lacking in the It.'[7]

In the perceptual process that differentiates the I from the It, a key role is played by the body. Pain gives us a special knowledge of our body. And our body is unique in being perceived from outside and from inside. Freud says:

The I is first and foremost a bodily I; it is not merely a surface entity, but is itself a projection of a surface (i.e. the I is ultimately derived from bodily sensations, chiefly those springing from the surface of the body. It may thus be regarded as a mental projection of the surface of the body . . .)[8]

The It is dominated by instincts and the pursuit of pleasure, while the I is concerned with self-preservation. Being formed around the perceptual system, the I is aware of the constraints of reality, and tries to replace blind instinctive action by coherent rational plans. But there are severe limits to how far the drives of the It can be constrained within the plans of the I. Freud likens the relation between the I and the It to a man on horseback, who has to hold in check the superior strength of the horse. He remarks that 'often a rider, if he is not to be parted from his horse, is obliged to guide it where it wants to go'.[9]

We might expect Freud to see the I as essentially a conscious centre of control. But he thinks that large parts of the I are normally unconscious. His argument for this appeals to the unconscious resistance he says is shown towards some topics by psychoanalytic patients. They are unaware of wanting to avoid these sensitive topics, but raising them makes associations fail or become irrelevant. Freud says the unconscious resistance cannot come from repressed material in the It, because 'we must rather attribute to the repressed a strong upward drive, an impulse to break through into consciousness'.[10] He concludes that it must be the unconscious work of the I. (It is an example of Freud's holism that this argument depends on his view that repressed material struggles towards consciousness.) The unconscious parts of the I differ from the It in not being primitive and irrational.

[7] New Introductory Lectures, Lecture 31.
[8] The Ego and the Id, translated by Joan Riviere, London, 1927, chapter 2.
[9] Ibid.
[10] New Introductory Lectures, Lecture 31.

The I has the problem of mediating between the desires of the It and the external world. Defences are needed, both against external threats and against the excessive demands of the instincts. Where satisfying these demands involves danger, the I may deal with the conflict by splitting, both recognizing and denying the danger at the same time.

Freud cites a case to illustrate this splitting.[11] A three-year-old boy discovered the female genitals as a result of being seduced by an older girl. Later on his nurse found him masturbating and threatened that his father would castrate him. (Did Freud's patients have unusually Freudian childhoods, or is it just that you had a very dull one?) Freud thinks that, having seen the girl, the boy would think of castration as a real possibility. The boy, however, pushed this threat from consciousness. 'He created a substitute for the penis which he missed in females – that is to say a fetish.' Released from what made the castration threat seem plausible, the boy continued to masturbate. Yet his denial was not complete. He showed that at some level he did accept the threat by developing an intense fear of being punished by his father, and an anxiety about either of his two smallest toes being touched.

(Once again, Freud's holism creates problems. The case history comes to us already interpreted in the light of the theory. It is less impressive as a case of splitting if we are sceptical about treating the toes as a penis substitute, and this applies even more to the same interpretation of the 'fetish', of which no other details are given.)

Freud sees this type of childhood conflict as causing 'a rift in the I which never heals but which increases as time goes on'. (This fits well with the studies suggesting that multiple personality is linked with having been a victim of child abuse.)

Related to splitting are other defence mechanisms used by the I, such as those Freud calls 'derealization' and 'depersonalization'.[12] Derealization involves a feeling that some part of what is being experienced cannot be real. Depersonalization is when part of one's own self feels alien. Freud suggests that derealization may be the I's defensive response to an external threat, while depersonalization may be a defence against inner thoughts and impulses. The general pattern of the I defending itself by altering the boundary between itself and the world is central to Freud's account of the origin of conscience. Parental disapproval is internalized and the inner parental voice is set up as something independent, in conflict with the I.

Freud saw the I as extending its influence over more of the It, replacing impulsive action by self-knowledge and coherent plans. He thought of psychoanalysis as providing help for the I. Greater understanding would strengthen the I, both against the inner parental voice and against the compulsions of the It.

Eliminating the spatial metaphors

A lot of this account uses spatial imagery. The I is on the surface of the It, although the lower part merges into the It. Repressed material pushes upwards towards the surface. The I splits in half. Freud sometimes seems to treat all this as metaphor and sometimes intends it literally.

The literal version is a set of neurophysiological hypotheses about localization in the brain, with the It in the middle and the I in the 'cortical layer' round the edge. Even now we have only a moderate knowledge of the parts of the brain active in complex mental functions. In Freud's time less was known, and his speculations on the topic are of no special value. The interest of his theory of the I is independent of which regions of the brain are involved. We have good reasons to discard the literal version.

There is then the problem of how to interpret the metaphorical version. We are left with a theory of the function and development of the I. If the I is not a region of the brain, what is it? Is it anything at all, or is it as mythical as the Cartesian ego?

The theory has two main components. One is the view that the emergence of the I is the development of a control centre, conscious of perceptual information, and which organizes action in the light of what is perceived. The second is about the role of the body in our conception of ourselves.

The account of the role of the body makes a Kantian point about awareness of personal frontiers, together with a point about mental images.

To form a conception of myself, I have to contrast myself with the rest of the world, which involves knowing where my boundaries come. Freud rightly cites two special features of my body, its sensitivity to pain, and its being perceived from inside as well as from outside, as relevant to the childhood discovery that its limits are also mine. He goes on to make a second point about the way a person's control centre uses imagery to include that person in its representation of the world. When Freud, having said that the I is derived from bodily sensations, continues that it is 'a mental projection of the surface of the body', he does not mean that the control centre *is* images of the body. In making plans, I have to think of myself as well as of the world in whch I act, and Freud believes I use images of the body to do this.

There are questions which could be asked about these images. Are they visual, tactile, or both? If they are visual, is the body seen from outside, or from the perspective of my own eyes, or does it shift between the two? Are the answers to these questions the same for everyone? Is there evidence that we use bodily images to think of ourselves? (Our doing so does not just follow from the Kantian point about the awareness of the bodily frontier being needed for self-consciousness.) Or is it just that it is hard to see what, apart from bodily images, we could use to represent ourselves? (This assumes that representation without images is impossible.)

But all this can be ignored here. The more interesting question is about what it is for the I to exercise control.

The control centre

The I controls actions, but like a man on horseback, taking account of where the horse wants to go. It also controls thoughts, again with only partial success, so that directed thinking contrasts with the tune I cannot get out of my head, the involuntary memory or the sudden impulsive desire. The I tries to impose decisions shaped by the constraints of reality on the It's pursuit of immediate pleasure.

The I, interpreted as a centre of reason's control over unruly desires, may seem like Kant's 'rational will'. In the Kantian picture, the will can intervene to motivate decisions independently of any desires the person may have. We have seen that this rather metaphysical force is hard to believe in. Freud's I is only of interest if it avoids the emptiness of the Cartesian ego. Seeing it as a control centre makes it a working part of our mental system rather than a detached metaphysical object. But if the control centre is a Kantian will, this advantage is lost. If the Freudian I is to avoid the problems of the rational will, its decisions have to be seen as motivated by desires. It has to restrain some desires in order to carry out plans motivated by others.

Being motivated by some desires to restrain others is part of everyday life. It happens when someone refuses a drink because of driving. The desire to avoid having a car crash or being arrested is stronger than the desire for a drink. For this we can again use the model of a committee, but one operating by majority vote, with no one in the chair. The committee may be dominated by different factions at different times, and so reach very different decisions. When I take a decision, *I* am not using the casting vote from the chair, but should be seen as the whole committee.

Many cases fit this picture of decisions being dominated by strongest desires. But it may be questioned whether in *all* cases *I* am just the committee of competing desires. A decision may involve weakness of will: I have decided to give up smoking but give way to the desire for a cigarette. It is sometimes said that, in such a case, what I do is not what I most want to do. Perhaps it is more plausible to say that the action I later regret was the one which *at that moment* I most wanted to do. Perhaps most of the time the desire to give up smoking is strongest, but at the time of weak-willed decision the desire for a cigarette is even stronger. Any other view has a problem explaining how the relative strength of desires can be assessed, apart from seeing which prevails in a conflict.

It is plausible, then, that even when I betray my long-term projects, my action does reflect the strength of my desires at that time. But, if so, there is something inadequate about identifying *me* with that pattern of desires. I have 'second-order desires': desires to have or not to have certain desires, and desires about which desires should prevail.

The incompleteness of seeing me simply in terms of the desires expressed in my choices (what economists call my 'revealed preference') is brought out by Harry Frankfurt's idea of a 'wanton'.[13] Wantons have only first-order desires. They are not glad or sorry to have those desires, and do not care which are expressed in their choices: the strongest desire dominates, and that is all there is to it. Wantons cannot have the longer-term plans which make us hope that some of our desires will prevail over others.

These psychological complications that mark us off from wantons generate the need for a control centre, restraining immediate impulses. Reverting to the model of a committee, this development enlarges the committee by including as voting members the desires caused by our plans and projects. (Including these desires in the committee is of course no guarantee that they will prevail.)

Depersonalization and splitting
==

So far in this discussion, there has been no suggestion that loss of control (where the horse runs away with the rider) involves any denial that the action is mine. I may regret doing something, while accepting that it was I who did it. But in more extreme cases there can be a more drastic repudiation. We have seen how, in certain neurological disorders, people feel no sense of ownership over parts of their own bodies. There can be a similar sense of alienation from one's own actions or psychological states. Freud says of this depersonalization that 'the subject feels . . . that a piece of his own self is strange to him'. He links it with split personality and suggests it is a defence mechanism used by the I against threats 'from the internal world of thoughts and impulses'.

When something is explained as a defence mechanism, it is not always made clear against what kind of threat the defence is being built. Sometimes the rejection of information can be a defence against a threat to efficient action: a writer may leave letters about his bank balance unopened because being depressed about money would hinder his work. Sometimes it can be a defence against mental pain:

[13] Harry Frankfurt: Freedom of the Will and the Concept of a Person, *Journal of Philosophy*, 1970.

people often 'cannot believe it' when someone close to them has just died, and doctors are familiar with the denial of a serious illness by a patient who has been told about it. And sometimes the defence is against a threat to a person's self-image.

Freud's example of a defence mechanism leading to splitting is one where the threat is painful anxiety about castration. (Denial of the threat is not a defence against castration itself, but only works against the anxiety.) He thinks the I splits, with one part recognizing the threat and one part denying it. We have seen that one case described by Freud is inconclusive as evidence of this splitting. But there are instances, not drawn from psychoanalytic cases, which can plausibly be interpreted along similar lines. The double life of bigamists or spies, and of the family man who works as a torturer, may involve something like Freudian splitting. Some of these are defences against threats to self-image. None of them seems to create in the different parts of the person complete mutual obliviousness. There is not the amnesia of multiple personality or the watertight barrier of the split brain patient.

In the type of case Freud cites, it again seems unlikely that the 'splitting' involves two non-communicating centres of consciousness on the split brain model. Some of the behaviour of the boy suggests belief in the castration threat, while some of it suggests disbelief. The plausible alternatives seem to be either some kind of conscious half-belief (perhaps a conscious oscillation between belief and disbelief) or else conscious disbelief combined with an unconscious tendency to believe. The case of half-belief or oscillation is hardly a very interesting form of splitting. The other case, of an unconscious tendency to believe, does involve some splitting of control, as conflicting plans are made on the basis of conflicting beliefs. But this conception of splitting must apply to a rather wide range of Freudian phenomena: wherever unconscious desires or beliefs push in the opposite way to conscious ones.

Draining the Zuyder Zee

Freud says of the I that 'starting from conscious perception, it has subjected to its influence ever larger regions and deeper strata of the

It'.[14] He sees this as a process which can be continued, partly with the help of psychoanalysis, whose intention he describes as being to strengthen the I: 'to widen its field of perception and enlarge its field of organization, so that it can appropriate fresh portions of the It. Where It was, there I shall be. It is a work of culture, not unlike the draining of the Zuyder Zee'.[15]

This process of land reclamation is a matter of uncovering and criticizing the unconscious or irrational parts of ourselves, so that our lives can be brought more under the control of our central desires.

There are two versions of this project, which result from Freud oscillating between two different accounts of the It. In *New Introductory Lectures on Psychoanalysis*, he argues that parts of the I are, like the It, unconscious. The It is marked off from those parts of the I by its 'primitive and irrational characteristics'.[16] But in *An Outline of Psychoanalysis*, he says that 'the sole prevailing quality of the It is that of being unconscious'.[17] When irrationality is seen as the key feature of the It, the aim that 'where It was, there I shall be' will be realized by weakening the power of irrational impulses over us. On the other interpretation of the It, the project will be one of making us conscious of what is now unconscious.

It is the 'bringing to consciousness' version of the project that has dominated psychoanalysis. The attempt has been to help bring repressed memories and desires to consciousness, and so to free people from the compulsions and distortions caused by this unconscious material. It is an empirical question how far psychoanalysis succeeds in bringing to consciousness what has been repressed. It is also an empirical question how far bringing it to consciousness gives any release from its power. It is possible that psychoanalysis succeeds on both these counts. But another possibility is that slavery to irrational impulses with an obscure unconscious basis is replaced by slavery to well-understood ones.

There may be a causal link such that exposing the unconscious origin of an impulse immediately weakens its grip on us. Or else making the origin conscious may make possible the kind of criticism that will weaken the impulse. But this is to move over to the other

[14] *An Outline of Psychoanalysis*, chapter 8.
[15] *New Introductory Lectures*, Lecture 31.
[16] Ibid.
[17] *An Outline of Psychoanalysis*, chapter 4.

version of the project, where land is reclaimed from irrationality rather than from unconsciousness. This second version of the colonizing of the It by the I is not elaborated by Freud, who seems to assume that unconscious irrational states will no longer enslave us when they are made conscious. If this is too optimistic, Freud's account of our taking control of our lives has a gap, waiting to be filled by an account of how to escape from the slavery imposed by conscious irrationality.

But, even if incomplete, Freud's account of the reclamation project is one of people taking charge of their lives. It is notable for its emphasis on this as an active, purposive process. A self-conscious and physically active person could, like Frankfurt's wanton, be psychologically passive. Such a person would act on desires, but they would all be seen as unalterable external forces, like the weather. I might find myself in a sudden gale of desires. I would be buffeted about, blown one way and then another, until the strongest finally determined which way I would act. But this is not Freud's picture. He sees that we can to some extent take charge of our lives, actively shaping ourselves and our desires according to our own plans. It is the great contribution of his theory of the I that he gives us this active role without the metaphysics of the rational will, but as part of a determinist model, in which our actions are still caused by our desires.

The ego from Descartes to Freud

Folk psychology, in which 'I' is a central concept, is sometimes thought static. Yet it is possible to see a little progress in the period from Descartes to Freud.

Descartes, for reasons we can understand, thought that 'I' refers to a metaphysical ego, whose existence we are infallibly aware of. But the Cartesian ego is not empirically detectable, and explains nothing. Hume and Kant, in different ways, both saw that we are not aware of the ego.

Hume saw people as part of the causally determined natural world. For him, 'I' does not refer to an ego that owns experiences, but refers simply to the causally connected series of experiences. 'My' actions are the causal product of my desires, which, unless they are based on false beliefs, are not open to rational criticism.

Kant agreed that we are not aware of the ego, but unhelpfully thought this is because it inhabits an unknowable 'noumenal' realm. He saw that self-awareness requires a contrast between me and the rest of the world, but was unclear about the frontier. He saw that the desires motivating an action can be rationally criticized. But he, again unhelpfully, thought reason was able to motivate action independently of any desires.

Freud followed Kant in seeing that I must be aware of a frontier between myself and other things. But he avoided the Cartesian side of Kant, and accepted the bodily frontier. He followed Hume in accepting that actions are caused by desires, and that decisions to act are not taken by a 'will' that escapes the causal process. But, unlike Hume, he saw that I can subject even my strongest present desire to rational criticism. This criticism is not free-floating: it is based on other desires. Those desires have to do with the conception I have of the life I want and the sort of person I want to be. Seeing the importance of these desires enables Freud, while accepting that what we do is causally determined, to stress that we can be active in taking charge of our lives.

CHAPTER THIRTEEN

PROJECTS
OF SELF-CREATION

One thing is needful. – To 'give style' to one's character – a great and rare art! It is practised by those who survey all the strengths and weaknesses of their nature and then fit them into an artistic plan until every one of them appears as art and reason and even weaknesses delight the eye. Here a large mass of second nature has been added; there a piece of original nature has been removed – both times through long practice and daily work at it. Here the ugly that could not be removed is concealed; there it has been reinterpreted and made sublime . . . In the end, when the work is finished, it becomes evident how the constraint of a single taste governed everything large and small. Whether this taste was good or bad is less important than one might suppose, if only it was a single taste!

FRIEDRICH NIETZSCHE: *The Gay Science.*

To VARYING DEGREES we take charge of our lives. Through controlling our actions by our own plans, we become active rather than passive. We may hardly notice changes taking place in ourselves, through being absorbed in what we are doing. But sometimes we are more self-conscious, and this starts to change us. We form pictures of the sort of person we want to be. Someone may want to be braver, more tolerant, more independent or less lazy. Consciously shaping our own characteristics is self-creation.

There may be a biological origin of our interest in developing our own individuality. Our pattern of sexual reproduction usually involves leaving the family group in which we were reared and developing a very intense interest in another person. Differentiating yourself from the rest of your family may be a psychological preparation for leaving it, as well as being a way of developing the features that will bond with those of your future partner. But members of other species also pair up, often apparently without any particular interest in self-creation. If this speculation about biological origins is right, humans have characteristically developed an elaborated version of self-differentiation, going beyond the minimal requirements of its original function.

It may seem that self-creation is something only a few people care about. Few of us are as heroic or as self-absorbed as the Nietzschean superman. Most of us do not spend our lives on endless landscape-gardening of the self. Many of us lead rather undramatic lives. The identity we create is often shaped, not by some heroic struggle, but through our choice of partners and friends, by the job we choose, and by where we decide to live.

But, in less strenuous form than Nietzsche envisaged, self-creation is almost universal. We take it for granted, until it is threatened. You are offered an interesting job, but on condition that your employer will take over some of the more personal aspects of your life. The employer will drastically change your clothes, your hairstyle, and the pictures and objects you have in your room. Your employer does not like your accent, and will have you taught to speak differently. You tend to slouch, and your facial expression is insufficiently pleasing. All this will be taken in hand too. If you now have second thoughts about the job, perhaps it is because you like to be the one who is in charge of these aspects of yourself.

Taking such decisions for yourself is self-creation. Perhaps it is a bit pretentious to give this title to attempts to become the sort of person who replies to letters. But the label will do, and these humdrum efforts at self-creation are probably at least as common as the more heroic feats. Self-creation is a matter of shaping our characteristics, even minor ones, in the light of our attitudes and values.

Self-creation can be thought of more broadly than in terms of active change. There is a 'conservative' version, which is less like an adolescent upheaval, and more a matter of maintaining yourself roughly as you are. The middle-aged refusal to take a different job, because of the kind of person you would become, is still a self-creative decision, if not a very exciting one.

Work
==

Self-creation can take place without being at the front of conscious-ness. Many people partly create themselves through their work. But this is normally an unself-conscious process. We strive for goals outside ourselves, and influence ourselves obliquely. But when work has been done for its own sake, we may later come to see how much of ourselves has been bound up in it. William James, talking about the destruction of a life's work, such as a butterfly collection or a book in manuscript, says that when such a disaster happens to us we feel 'a sense of the shrinkage of our personality, a partial conversion of ourselves to nothingness'.[1]

Work does not always help self-creation. Deadening work, done only to earn a living, may also shape us, but not in ways we would choose. And some work done for its own sake may be chosen at some sacrifice of self-creation. A novel or a discovery in science may have a price, which the novelist or scientist pays in becoming narrow, oblivious and selfish. A politician may find he can only further his ideals by making shabby compromises along the way.

> The intellect of man is forced to choose
> Perfection of the life or of the work,
> And if it take the second must refuse
> A heavenly mansion, raging in the dark.

W. B. YEATS: *The Choice.*

Although not all work helps self-creation, to many people it is important to have the chance of the kind of work which does. If self-creation is important to us, the availability of such work may be more important than other economic goals which are often put before it. Not everyone wants to work. But often people who do are excluded from work, or forced to earn a living by doing things they find futile.

Now that we can develop machines to do the boring jobs, we can choose how to use this power. We could put first an ever-rising 'standard of living', always aiming for more and better goods. The cycle of each year producing more and consuming more can go on

[1] William James: *The Principles of Psychology*, volume 1, page 293.

as long as people can be persuaded to do both. Or we could put first the creation of satisfying work for those who want it, even if there were some economic cost. If we are lucky, there may be no economic cost: perhaps the most satisfying work happens to provide goods and services people most want in the most efficient way. But perhaps there is a conflict. If so, becoming conscious of the more subtle aspects of our own psychology may make us more inclined to shape society round these needs rather than round ever higher levels of consumption.

Style
==

It was lunch at the Goethes', and Goethe himself was quiet,

... no doubt so as not to disturb the free speech of his very voluble and logically penetrating guest, who elaborated upon himself in oddly complicated grammatical forms. An entirely novel terminology, a mode of expression mentally overleaping itself, the peculiarly employed philosophical formulas of the ever more animated man in the course of his demonstrations – all this finally reduced Goethe to complete silence without the guest even noticing ...

One of the others at the meal said afterwards,

'I cannot tell whether he is brilliant or mad. He seems to me to be an unclear thinker.'[2]

This response to Hegel's lunchtime conversation will strike a sympathetic note in many who have tried to read his books. The Hegelian style is not easily missed.

Out of a mixture of natural development and conscious choices, people develop a distinctive style that can be their most recognizable feature.

Oliver Sacks describes how people immobilized for years with severe Parkinson's disease could respond to treatment with L-dopa by an awakening in which their original personal style was apparent. He says the same can be true of patients with dementias, in whom can sometimes be seen 'vivid, momentary recalls of the original, lost person', and concludes: 'style, in short, is the deepest thing in one's being'.[3]

[2] The description is by Ottilie von Goethe, quoted in Geoffrey Hawthorn: *Hegel's Odyssey*, *London Review of Books*, October, 1985.
[3] Oliver Sacks: *Awakenings*, Harmondsworth, 1976, page 278.

Style combines chosen forms of self-expression with what we are given naturally. The way people do things is partly chosen. But Nietzsche's advice about the cultivation of a style, if too consciously followed, could produce mere affectation. (Nietzsche sometimes seems to have been an eternal first-year undergraduate.)

Avoiding some exaggerations

The idea of self-creation needs disentangling from some exaggerations. A project of self-creation need not be the most important thing in someone's life. It is possible to care about what sort of person you are becoming, but to think other things matter more. ('This job is deadening my imagination, but the alternative is unemployment.')

To have a project of self-creation need not involve a 'life plan': a unitary blueprint of how your life is supposed to turn out. A few people have such plans. But probably, for most of us, self-creation is a matter of a fairly disorganized cluster of smaller aims: more like building a medieval town than a planned garden city.

We need not overrate our powers of self-creation. In the first place, there are logical limits to what we can do. It is self-defeating to aim directly at being more spontaneous or less self-conscious. These aims can be realized, if at all, only by oblique strategies. And with some other states, we can aim directly at them, but awareness of success is destabilizing. One case is the religious problem about knowing you are really humble.

There are also severe factual limits to our powers. Some philosophers have talked as if our characteristics, or at least our psychological characteristics, were entirely under our control. Sartre, in his early writings, is an example. But later he came to think differently:

Then, little by little, I found that the world was more complicated than this, for during the Resistance there appeared to be a possibility of free decision . . . The other day I reread a prefatory note of mine to a collection of these plays . . . and was truly scandalized. I had written: 'Whatever the circumstances, and wherever the site, a man is always free to choose to be a traitor or not . . .' When I read this, I said to myself: It's incredible, I actually believed that![4]

[4] Jean-Paul Sartre: The Itinerary of a Thought, in *Between Existentialism and Marxism*, London, 1974.

No doubt we sometimes deceive ourselves, treating characteristics, which could with some effort be changed, as unalterable facts independent of our will. (People are rightly suspicious when someone complacently says, 'I just am a lazy person.') But it is absurd to suppose that all our psychological characteristics can be altered substantially and at will, or even that more than a few can be entirely altered. Anyone who thinks so should talk to people who seek help in changing themselves from psychoanalysts or behaviour therapists.

On the other hand, not all self-creation involves strenuous efforts of will. It can be a matter of endorsing and encouraging tendencies that are already natural to us. We may be endorsing something which has cost us no effort to produce, but with which we feel an immediate affinity. (I have heard that Picasso, when asked to sign paintings thought to be his, would sign if he liked the painting, even if unsure that it was his work.)

Self-creation may not need either strenuous effort or the instant malleability of our whole character. It is a platitude that, for most people, some traits are virtually unalterable, and that some others can be altered only by drastic changes in way of life, or by effort over time. Self-creation is not like the instantaneous transformations of magic, but more like sculpting a piece of wood, respecting the constraints of natural shape and grain.

'The real me'

We discover these natural constraints as we try things out. Work, again, can help us discover ourselves. It is put well by a character in *Heart of Darkness*:

'No, I don't like work. I had rather laze about and think of all the fine things that can be done. I don't like work, – no man does – but I like what is in the work, – the chance to find yourself. Your own reality – for yourself, not for others – what no other man can ever know. They can only see the mere show, and never can tell what it really means.'[5]

We are lucky if work brings out in us things we did not know we had. But we can also discover things about ourselves in a less

[5] Joseph Conrad: *Heart of Darkness*, Harmondsworth, 1973, page 41.

satisfying way. We take a job because it is well paid, or because others find it interesting, and then find we are stifled by it. Parts of us are denied expression. ('It was not really me', we say afterwards.) Relationships lead to the same kind of self-discovery: in some we flourish and in some we are stifled.

The experience of recognizing what suits our own nature was well described by William James, in a letter to his wife: 'A man's character is discernible in the mental or moral attitude in which, when it came upon him, he felt himself most deeply and intensely active and alive. At such moments there is a voice inside which speaks and says: "This is the real me!"'[6]

This is an experience many people have. But what we are aware of at such moments needs an explanation which our present knowledge cannot provide. How does it come about that we have these natural affinities?

When a way of life does not fit with what you think you are really like, you can feel like a plant away from the light, distorted by having to twist and grope towards the sun. This analogy suggests that we might have a genetic programme to unfold, in the way plants do. But no doubt it is too simple to think that 'the real me' is genetically laid down. These strong affinities we have for some kinds of life, and the sense of drowning that others give us, are likely to have been created by the interaction of our genetic make-up with things we have come across and responded to.

This strong sense of a natural line of development is a striking feature of people. We might not have been like this. People might have been much more adaptable and interchangeable. Perhaps these individual differences in part reflect the diversity of the human gene pool. But we have little understanding of how genes and experiences interact in this: to programme a person to feel drawn towards one kind of life and so intensely uncomfortable with others. How this happens is a question for the more developed psychology or neuroscience of the future.

[6] *The Letters of William James*, ed. Henry James, London, 1920, volume I, page 199.

Three entangled processes
===

What people become depends partly on things quite outside themselves. But it is also the product of three internally generated processes.

There is the genetically programmed cycle of life, which we can hardly alter. We do not choose the dependence of childhood, the emotional upheaval of adolescence, or the slow downhill drift of middle age and beyond. The general shape is the unfolding of a fixed programme like that of a plant or tree.

Then there is the unself-conscious process of living our lives: we choose a job because it sounds interesting, or live somewhere because it is near our work, and changes in us are the unintended result of these choices. Many things that people do have such unintended self-creative side effects.

The third process is deliberate self-creation.

These processes are so entangled that it is often quite obscure which changes came about because of choices and which were part of the unfolding programme. We are a bit like trees would be, if they were conscious and could partly choose their direction of growth. Perhaps oaks could not become beeches, and stunted trees could not become giants, but they could influence the angle and direction of their branches. Trees thinking about determinism and free will might find it impossible to assess their own contribution to their final shape. (This uncertainty also holds for our estimate of our influence on others, as parents know.)

CHAPTER FOURTEEN

THE INNER STORY

> Truly, though our element is time,
> We are not suited to the long perspectives
> Open at each instant of our lives.
> They link us to our losses: worse,
> They show us what we have as it once was,
> Blindingly undiminished, just as though
> By acting differently we could have kept it so.
>
> PHILIP LARKIN: *Reference Back.*

SELF-CREATION DEPENDS on the beliefs we have about what we are now like: on the stories we tell about ourselves. We tell other people what to expect of us, or else we send signals by actions or style. The stories vary. Applying for a job, we tell a story about our competence and energy, about how we have always cared more about Quantity Surveying than about anything else in the world. To our family and our friends we tell stories ranging over more of our life. But we also tell ourselves a story about ourselves. This is our inner story. It stretches back as far as we can remember. We think of it as the truth from which other stories may deviate a bit.

We simplify when we think of the inner story as the truth. What we tell ourselves is not the whole story, as an objective God might tell it. Such a God would include our unconscious motives, and the story would not have items left out or distorted through forgetting or bias. (One reason why Tolstoy gives the impression of writing like God is that he both lets us see more about his characters than they do themselves, and at the same time gives us access to the inner story of many of them.)

Many projects of self-creation can only be understood in the light of the inner story of which they are part. My attitudes towards my past influence, and are influenced by, what I want to become. Both the content and the emotional tone of the story so far make intentions about the next part more intelligible.

H.M.

Some ways in which memory contributes to identity can be seen through the devastation caused by its loss. One of the most fully described cases is that of 'H.M.', whose memory impairment resulted from a brain operation he had as a young man in 1953.[1] H.M. has no loss of early memories, and only some impairment of memory for events shortly before the operation. His striking defect is an inability to store new memories.

An early neurological account brings out the scale of H.M.'s impairment.

Ten months ago the family moved from their old house to a new one a few blocks away on the same street; he still has not learned the new address, though remembering the old one perfectly, nor can he be trusted to find his way home alone . . . His mother still has to tell him where to find the lawn mower, even though he may have been using it only the day before. She also states that he will do the same jigsaw puzzles day after day without showing any practice effect and that he will read the same magazines over and over again without finding their contents familiar. This patient has even eaten luncheon in front of us . . . without being able to name, a mere half hour later, a single item of food he had eaten; in fact he could not remember having eaten luncheon at all.

Clearly this impairment would have devastating effects on the maintenance of a coherent personality. Coherence needs sequences of actions, planned as part of integrated projects. H.M. cannot build on the past. The monitoring of progress needed even for buying someone a birthday present depends on storing new memories. Trying to carry out a plan would be like building a tower out of dry sand, that trickles away as you heap it.

[1] W. B. Scoville and B. Milner: Loss of Recent Memory after Bilateral Hippocampal Lesions, *Journal of Neurology, Neurosurgery and Psychiatry*, 1957. The case is followed up in B. Milner, S. Corkin and H.-L. Teuber: Further Analysis of the Hippocampal Amnesic Syndrome: 14-Year Follow-Up Study of H.M., *Neuropsychologia*, 1968.

If all my memories were obliterated, this would obviously have a disastrous effect on my sense of who I am. My position would be worse than that of H.M. He at least has a conception of himself based on memories of what he was like before the operation. But total amnesia for my own past leaves me with a picture of myself as blank as the one people have on meeting me for the first time.

Memory does not wait to be consulted. Without conscious direction, it provides a stream of comparative information: 'the leaves are more autumnal than when we went away', 'she looks older, and she has grown much more self-confident', and so on. Memory helps to make us who we are, by giving us knowledge of the past and by underpinning projects over time. But the contribution of memory to our sense of ourselves goes further.

The loss of involuntarily produced comparisons is less catastrophic than loss of all access to the past. But the steady background awareness of similarities and contrasts given by normal memory contributes to our sense of the relative stability of the world. And it makes us aware of having a psychological trajectory as well as a physical one. (This is also helped by the way the almost total recall of what I did a moment ago fades without sharp boundary into the hazier recall of events further in the past.)

A store of memories is necessary for self-knowledge. And the process of involuntary comparison locates present experiences in their context of my past history. The interaction between self-creation and the inner story about the past helps answer one question about the special importance of memory for our conception of our own identity.

Charged memory

Some memories give information in a neutral way, about what I had for breakfast or about which year the house was painted. And even emotional episodes can often be recalled in a memory experience which is itself emotionally neutral. St Augustine found this puzzling, and explained it by likening memory to a sort of stomach for the mind, in which sweet or bitter food can be stored without its flavour being preserved. But he was still puzzled:

Perhaps these emotions are brought forward from the memory by the act of remembering in the same way as cattle bring up food from the stomach when they chew the cud. But if this is so, when a man discusses them – that is, when he recalls them to mind – why does he not experience the pleasure of joy or the pain of sorrow in his mind, just as the animal tastes the food in its mouth?[2]

But some memories themselves carry an emotional charge. These charged memories seem to be important to our sense of our identity, yet it is hard to say what their importance is.

One of Freud's central claims was that our most influential charged memories are often unconscious. An emotionally painful past experience, perhaps in childhood, has been repressed. But its presence is felt in the motivation of actions now. Someone punctilious to a neurotic degree, spending hours making his tax return accurate to the last penny, is perhaps unconsciously motivated. Suppose it can be shown that he has repressed a humiliating childhood experience of being caught stealing. His present behaviour can perhaps be interpreted as unconsciously motivated by the (impossible) desire to alter the past: to refute the childhood accusations of dishonesty. Freudians make the further claim that bringing the repressed memory to the surface in psychoanalysis can weaken its grip on our actions.

Perhaps a Freudian view of this sort is sometimes true. But such cases are not the only ones. Sometimes we are moulded by past events whose emotional impact we can remember quite clearly: a bereavement, a divorce, or an embarrassing involvement in a much-publicized scandal. And there are other cases of emotionally charged contact with our past where Freudian ideas about repression do not seem plausible. A place not visited since childhood, a taste or a smell, a distinctive tone of voice, can all trigger memories with a strong charge. Why does contact with a forgotten past sometimes evoke responses that seem to go so deep?

Proust's explanation
==

An account based on his own experiences of charged memory was put forward by Proust in the first volume of his autobiographical

[2] St Augustine: *Confessions*, translated by R. S. Pine-Coffin, Harmondsworth, 1961, Book 10, sections 8–21.

novel *Remembrance of Things Past*. On tasting a madeleine soaked in tea,

... an exquisite pleasure had invaded my senses, something isolated, detached, with no suggestion of its origin. And at once the vicissitudes of life had become indifferent to me, its disasters innocuous, its brevity illusory – this new sensation having had on me the effect which love has of filling me with a precious essence; or rather this essence was not in me, it *was* me.

It was hard to bring the origin of this feeling to consciousness, but then:

I place in position before my mind's eye the still recent taste of that first mouthful, and I feel something start within me, something that leaves its resting-place and attempts to rise, something that has been embedded like an anchor at a great depth ...[3]

After many attempts, there returned the memory of the madeleine dipped in tea given him as a boy by his aunt Léonie, and memories of his whole boyhood life came with it.

Proust reflects on the significance of these charged memories near the end of the novel, when others occur. The narrator wipes his mouth with a stiff napkin, triggering an old memory of visiting Balbec, where he had dried his face with a starchy towel by a window next to the beach. He is now able to analyse the emotional impact of such memories. What he found himself enjoying

... was not merely these colours but a whole instant of my life on whose summit they rested, an instant which had been no doubt an aspiration towards them and which some feeling of fatigue or sadness had perhaps prevented me from enjoying at Balbec but which now, freed from what is necessarily im-perfect in external perception, pure and disembodied, caused me to swell with happiness.[4]

Proust thinks the impact of memory is linked to leaving out the imperfections of reality. This may fit some cases but not all. A memory of a terrible experience can be strongly charged. And the emotional force may not even require eliminating minor irritations: we do not have to blank out the wasps that spoilt a childhood picnic.

But Proust's other thought is surely plausible: the object or scene remembered is valued less for its own sake than for the past context

[3] Marcel Proust: *Remembrance of Things Past*, translated by C. K. Scott Moncrieff and Terence Kilmartin, London, 1981, volume 1, pages 48–49.
[4] Ibid., volume 3, page 901.

it evokes. If a photograph of the scene at Balbec had been hanging on the wall for years, the association with the past would have been blurred by others, and the emotional charge would have been lost.

Proust says of such past contexts:

... the simplest act or gesture remains immured as within a thousand sealed vessels, each one of them filled with things of a colour, a scent, a temperature that are absolutely different one from another, vessels, moreover, which being disposed over the whole range of our years, during which we have never ceased to change if only in our dreams and our thoughts, are situated at the most various moral altitudes and give us the sensation of extraordinarily diverse atmospheres.[5]

The atmosphere of different stages of our life must contribute to the emotional charge of memories. But there is the further question: why should this be so? Memories of contexts with a different atmosphere, without the added dimension of time, can be quite neutral. At home for the weekend, someone may recall the very different atmosphere of a weekday place of work and be quite unmoved.

Proust gives an explanation of why recalling the atmosphere of a different time affects us:

I experienced them at the present moment and at the same time in the context of a distant moment, so that the past was made to encroach upon the present and I was made to doubt whether I was in the one or the other. The truth surely was that the being within me which had enjoyed these impressions had enjoyed them because they had in them something that was common to a day long past and to the present, because in some way they were extra-temporal, and this being made its appearance only when, through one of these identifications of the present with the past, it was likely to find itself in the one and only medium in which it could exist and enjoy the essence of things, that is to say: outside time.[6]

This explanation is useless. The mysterious extra-temporal 'being within me' is another appearance of the Cartesian ego or the Kantian 'noumenal self'. ('The being that thinks in us' is one of Kant's wilder phrases.) There is something right about the idea that our response to the 'various moral altitudes' is linked to our sense of our identity (that, as Proust said about his response to the madeleine, 'this essence

5 Ibid., volume 3, page 903.
6 Ibid., volume 3, page 904.

was not in me, it *was* me'). Can the idea be kept without this dubious commitment to the ego?

Past responses and the inner story

Replace Proust's upward metaphor of different altitudes with one going downwards. His investigation is a geology of the mind. A person can be seen as a deep-rooted tree, drawing nourishment from many different strata laid down in the past.

Why does awareness of the lower strata affect us emotionally? Surely in part because these events of long ago are remembered from a perspective inside myself as a participant, one that gives me access to my own emotions of that time. The taste or smell which triggers the memory may not originally have aroused any special emotional response, but experiencing it again gives some access to my emotional climate when I experienced it then.

This access is not just a matter of observing that emotional climate, but enables me to experience again some of those emotions, perhaps in a changed form or with different intensity. This may heighten my sympathy with my earlier self. (The way this happens is like the way I may come to identify with other people: awareness of their emotional states can cause similar emotions in me.)

It has been suggested that charged memories encapsulate something of our whole emotional history, from the remembered event to now. Richard Wollheim says that these memories reproduce the emotional tone of the original event, but also have had to compromise with other feelings and dispositions. He says,

The despair, the self-righteousness, the rage, that I experience when I remember my adolescent quarrel with my father represent the whole of me till now as well as me specifically then. It is thus that the affective tone of a memory comes to stand for a man's past as well as for one event in that past, and so when, by virtue of the key feature of mental connectedness, that tone casts its influence over the man, the man is thereby brought under the influence of the past generally as well as of some particular past event.[7]

[7] Richard Wollheim: Memory, Experiential Memory and Personal Identity, in G. F. Macdonald (ed.): *Perception and Identity, Essays Presented to A. J. Ayer*, London, 1979. The theme is also discussed in Richard Wollheim: *The Thread of Life*, Cambridge, Mass., 1984.

This picture of our whole past combining to influence us now is an attractive one. It makes memory like some casserole where the ingredients partly retain their identity and partly absorb the other flavours. But is it true? It is easy to see how one memory can become permeated by the flavour of another. Someone's first visit to Vienna may be exhilarating because of a love affair. Later and more prosaic visits there may raise the hope of recapturing that first magic, and memories of these visits may become fused with the earlier memories they evoked. But this is a special case. What about memories not consciously recalled in the intervening years? Has their emotional atmosphere mingled with that of others? Perhaps there has been unconscious permeation, but this would need some supporting evidence.

Part of the impact of these memories may result from the way they make it easier to see something of the pattern of the inner story.

When earlier events are relived in memory, they become more vivid, less obscured by more recent happenings, and the pattern of the inner story emerges more clearly. Recalling our own part in them, we can see ways in which we have changed, but we also come across actions and attitudes that would be natural to us still.

And when we remember something from long ago, we are going back to a time, and perhaps a place, where things were seen differently. In ways hard now to pin down, the beliefs, interests and values of people there were different. Compared to those you now meet, the people you knew then gave different kinds of stimulus and of emotional support. They made different emotional demands, and brought different pressures to bear. These contrasts show the choices you have made since then. (Perhaps they were your family, and wanted you to be a doctor, but you have become a journalist.) Now you have a different circle of friends, with a different emotional climate. Contact with the past is a reminder of alternatives to the present pattern of life. This sharpens awareness of the relationships you have helped to create, and of the pattern of your own life while doing so.

The memory trigger may also be reassuring about the objectivity of the inner story. Although we know that the earlier parts of our life were real, the parts we rehearse to ourselves can start to seem like private legends. To visit the place and find that it does look as remembered, or to have new detail unearthed in memory by a fresh external stimulus, is welcome corroboration. We may feel the kind of gratitude felt by believers in the Bible when archaeologists find evidence that there really was a Flood. If the inner story needs some correction, even this may confirm its status. It can be wrong because it is about things that really happened. Involuntary memories can confirm our sense of who we are by supporting the inner story we tell about ourselves.

The inner story as non-fiction

If our past can seem like fiction, something similar can happen to the present. People suffering from depersonalization lack the sense that what they do is an expression of themselves. And feelings of this sort are not confined to psychiatric patients. Children and adolescents can feel they have not developed characteristics which are really theirs. Sartre described this feature of his childhood:

My true self, my character and my name were in the hands of adults; I had learnt to see myself through their eyes; I was a child, this monster they were forming out of their regrets ... I was an impostor ... I went into the kitchen, announcing that I wanted to shake the salad; there would be cries and shrieks of laughter: 'No, darling, not like that! Hold your little hand tight: that's it! Marie, help him! Look how well he's doing it!' I was a bogus child holding a bogus salad basket; I could feel my actions changing into gestures.[8]

The same sense of our actions not expressing any distinctive characteristics of our own can arise in adult life. It can come when other people insist on telling our story for us in their terms, imposing their interpretation to 'explain' what we do.

At least since Freud, we have known that our picture of ourselves is sometimes distorted. We need no telling that this is true of other people's pictures of us. Apart from prejudice and lack of information, people are too busy, and do not want to study each other with the detailed attention that Proust gave to himself. We have only simplified sketches of each other, which leave out the fuzzy edges. We see people as kind or honest, when really they are almost always fairly kind, or honest except when ... We often know how our own supposed features have blurred edges, how they have fluctuated during the story, and how their continuation depends precariously

[8] Jean-Paul Sartre: *Words*, translated by Irene Clephane, Harmondsworth, 1967, page 54.

on our future decisions. So we sometimes wonder if we have these features at all.

Sartre describes his childhood sense of the contrast between the apparent stability of some other people's characteristics and the precariousness of his own:

Naturally I was able, when asked, to make known my preferences and even to insist on them; but when I was alone, they escaped me: far from being sure of them, I had to grip them, push them, breathe life into them; I was no longer even sure if I preferred beefsteak to roast veal. I would have given anything for some tortured landscape, with prejudices sheer as cliffs, to be installed in me.[9]

Usually we do not mind the simplified picture others have of us, as long as it is roughly right. But the pressure of expectations based on a false picture can be cramping and distorting. Or the picture may only be simplified, but in a way that invites self-caricature. Philip Larkin, explaining why he had not accepted to be a 'poet in residence', said, 'I did not want to go around pretending to be me.'

We can lose the sense that what we do is really part of our own story in other ways. Commitments to others can make us repeatedly defer what we ourselves most want to do. Parents (especially mothers) of young children often feel this. ('Something is pushing them to the side of their own lives.')

Something similar can happen through having to spend a lot of time adopting some other perspective. It is said that actors, after taking on a series of different personalities, can have a weakened sense of any features being distinctively theirs. The same can happen as the result of a novelist's or poet's sympathetic identification with other people. Keats wrote:

It is a wretched thing to confess; but it is a very fact that not one word I ever utter can be taken for granted as an opinion growing out of my identical nature – how can it, when I have no nature? When I am in a room with People if I ever am free from speculating on creations of my own brain, then not myself goes home to myself: but the identity of everyone in the room begins so to press upon me that, I am in a very little time annihilated . . .[10]

In these different ways we can come to feel we do not succeed in expressing ourselves in what we do. We feel that, in conforming to what people expect, we are acting out a piece of fiction. This contrasts with the story that others do not know: the inner story, which alone

[9] Ibid., pages 57–58.
[10] Robert Gittings (ed.): *Letters of John Keats*, Oxford, 1970, page 158.

is non-fiction. Or we feel that the development of the inner story is held up while we deal with things that are not part of it at all. Or, perhaps worst of all, we start to feel that we no longer have an inner story. But how can this be possible? If I am doing things, what can it mean to say that they are not part of my story?

Abridgment and editing

The inner story involves a good deal of selection. Jorge Luis Borges wrote a story about someone who remembered all the details of his past:

He knew by heart the forms of the southern clouds at dawn on 30 April 1882, and could compare them in his memory with the mottled streaks on a book in Spanish binding he had only seen once and with the outlines of the foam raised by an oar in the Rio Negro the night before the Quebracho uprising.[11]

Such a memory would be useless for finding your way about the past. Imagine going round a city with a map as large and as detailed as the place itself. We need an abridged version of memory.

Fortunately our memory is not like the one Borges described. In some of the classical studies of memory, people are told a story, and asked at intervals to reproduce it. As the original telling recedes further into the past, the reproduced version becomes more of a schematic outline, with ever fewer details.[12] Our grasp of the story of our own past depends on this largely unconscious process of abridgment.

This abridgment does not leave only generalities, but usually includes some striking details. When working well, it is like a good historian, who cannot tell us *everything* about the Mediterranean world of the sixteenth century, but uses telling detail to give an impression of the texture of that life.

To abridge the inner story is to edit it. The editing may take two forms. Wishful thinking, fantasy and self-deception may play their part: bits of the film we do not like are lost in the cutting room. This first kind of editing makes a gap between the inner story and how we really are.

The other kind of editing does not add or leave out any incidents,

[11] Jorge Luis Borges: Funes the Memorious, in *Labyrinths*, translated by Donald A. Yates and James E. Irby, Harmondsworth, 1970.
[12] Frederick Bartlett: *Remembering*, Cambridge, 1932.

but colours what happened by taking an attitude towards it. (It can be likened to adding the 'voice-over', or commentary.) I identify with some of the things I did but not with others, and, in presenting my past to myself, I give or withhold endorsement accordingly. Adding voice-over does not make the inner story inaccurate or incomplete. If someone else could have access to the inner story, this commentary would give them more understanding of my projects of self-creation.

Just as we do not always identify with past actions or motives, so we may not identify with things we do now. In a moment of weakness, you respond politely to a racist joke, and then feel a sense of betrayal. Perhaps at the moment of response your strongest desire is not to hurt the feelings of the person making the joke, or else to avoid the embarrassment that would follow the expression of your real attitude. As in other cases of weakness of will, it is plausible to suppose that you were acting on desires which were at that moment stronger than the countervailing ones.

This sort of case illustrates again the inadequacy of identifying *me* with my actions or with the desires that prevail in them. The thought that the polite response to the racist joke involves 'not being true to myself' is not misplaced. It is part of me that I feebly made the polite response, but the picture of me is incomplete without including the desires and values that were betrayed. It is mainly because our strongest desires are not always those we most identify with, that the 'revealed preferences' displayed in our choices do not always tell the whole story about us.

The vague phrase 'identifying with a desire' obscures a distinction between two kinds of identification. In one way, to identify with a desire is to think that acting on it will reflect what in general I most care about. But, in another way, identifying with a desire depends on its fitting my picture of the sort of person I want to be. These two kinds of identification may conflict.

A case of this conflict might arise for a political leader fighting an election whose outcome he thinks overwhelmingly important. (The rival party is a Nazi party, or is trigger-happy about nuclear weapons.) A scandal breaks about one of the political leader's friends. He has the decent instinct to speak out in defence of his friend. But he is warned (plausibly, let us suppose) that close association with his disgraced friend may lose his party the election. So, reluctantly, he **stays silent**. He does not want his desire to speak out to prevail, because he accepts the case for silence. So, in one way, he does not identify with the desire to speak out: it conflicts with what he most cares about. But, in another way, he does identify with that desire. He wants to be the sort of person who, under normal circumstances, will speak out on such an issue. He regards his present silence as a tactical retreat from this policy rather than as a permanent surrender. (The danger of self-deception hardly needs pointing out.) And in *this* sense of 'identification', he identifies with the first-order desire rather than with the considered judgment which prevails.

In these two different ways, I can repudiate what are, at the moment of choice, my strongest desires. Neither of these kinds of repudiation need involve denying that the action and its motives were mine. But, as we have seen, the editing of the inner story can go beyond loaded commentary and involve various kinds of denial of what I did. The mildest form goes only a little beyond the repudiation we have been considering. It is the compartmentalization that shields us from emotional awareness of what we do: a simple case is the way those of us who eat meat shy away from visiting or imagining factory farms and slaughterhouses. A stronger version is found in the 'doubling' perhaps characteristic of some torturers: from the perspective of the family man at home, the other episodes seem to belong to the life of someone else.

In doubling, whole strands of what happened are excluded from the inner story. But the editing can work the other way, so that my identifications become broader rather than narrower. When people write autobiographies, the broad or narrow boundaries of their self-conception are often on display. Sometimes the story of *my* life is literally that: I did this, then I did that, then I did the other. But, in other autobiographies, the story of my life is impossible to disentangle from the ups and downs of the family and friends I am involved with, the causes I believe in, or the neighbourhood where I feel I belong. This may be just a sympathetic concern for others, but it can be something stronger and more personal. If you are personally affronted on hearing your friends, your race or your religion disparaged, your inner story is a less narrow one, because your attitude to these groups goes beyond sympathy to identification.

These various kinds of identification or repudiation are what the editing of the inner story consists in. And projects of self-creation can often be understood only in the context of the story as edited so far. This is because of the way the voice-over about the past shades into a running commentary on the present. In a chapter of a novel, the actions make sense because of the previous chapters. And the coherence of an account by a single person is crucial here. A chapter from one of the books of *The Raj Quartet* would have a different meaning if the events of the previous chapters had been described, not by Paul Scott, but by Rudyard Kipling. One reason why the inner story up to now is relevant to understanding present actions is that self-creation tends to make a life like a novel by a single author.

The inner story and self-creation

There is a need for an inner story. Some evidence is provided by people who, deprived of their own inner story, confabulate a succession of stories instead. Oliver Sacks describes 'Mr Thompson', whose memory of his past had been destroyed by Korsakov's syndrome, and who constantly invented different pasts for himself. Sacks says that his situation is terrible: 'For here is a man who, in some sense, is desperate, in a frenzy . . . He must seek meaning, *make* meaning, in a desperate way, continually inventing . . .'[13] Our inner story lets us get our bearings when we act. Without it, all decisions would be like steering at sea without a map or compass. It is not surprising if those without a story are driven to invention.

Charles Taylor has argued that man is a self-interpreting animal.[14] The way we think of ourselves helps to shape what we are like. This influence is peculiarly direct. It is not like the way we are affected by others' view of us. I can be influenced by your picture of me, perhaps trying to fit myself to it, or perhaps trying to prove it wrong. But the influence of my own view of myself is more immediate.

There are several ways in which my thoughts about myself affect what I am like. One is that my mental states can partly depend on what I believe them to be. This is what makes it absurd when a Christian Scientist says that pain is an illusion, and that no one really

---

[13] Oliver Sacks: *The Man Who Mistook His Wife for a Hat*, London, 1985.
[14] Charles Taylor: Self-interpreting Animals, in *Human Agency and Language, Philosophical Papers*, 1, Cambridge, 1985.

suffers it. If I feel as if I am in pain, this is (at least) a large part of *being* in pain. Some other mental states have the same feature. If I think I am embarrassed, I am embarrassed.

This point about mental states is hard to pin down precisely. It is a mistake to think of our mental states as existing, like physical objects, in a way that is quite independent of our beliefs about them. But it is also wrong to suggest that the nature of our mental states depends entirely on our beliefs about them. If I think I am not jealous, I may be mistaken. And mental states vary in how belief-dependent they are. There is more scope for being wrong about whether I am jealous than about whether I am embarrassed or amused.

How I think of myself also affects the choices I make. Suppose I am offered a job as presenter of a television programme, in which people compete for refrigerators and washing-machines by guessing their price. My role would be to describe the prizes in a drooling voice, and then to jolly the contestants into smiles and chat. If I see myself as a rising star in show-business, I may take it on. But other kinds of self-conception might have a different result. (Imagine Kierkegaard being offered the job.)

My view of myself affects what I do, and is bound up with how I see my story so far. This is one reason why psychoanalysis and similar techniques might change people. Psychoanalysis can be seen as a way of getting you to rewrite the inner story so far. To get the story rewritten, the claim has to be made that the new version is nearer the truth, but the rewriting may be effective even if the claim is unfounded. Rewriting the story can change the context and direction of self-creation.

It is not only in psychoanalysis that talk affects self-creation. The story of my past merges into the commentary I make on the present. And this commentary is not just inner monologue, but is partly created when we talk to each other. This talk, when we share what we have been doing and our responses to things that have happened, is not just an exchange of information. When we talk together, I learn from your way of seeing things, which will often be different from mine. And, when I tell you about my way of seeing things, I am not just describing responses that are already complete. They may only emerge clearly as I try to express them, and as I compare them with yours. In this way, we can share in the telling of each other's inner story, and so share in creating ourselves and each other.

CHAPTER FIFTEEN

====

BELIEF

BELIEFS ABOUT myself and my history are not the only ones with a part in self-creation. We define ourselves partly by our distinctive beliefs about the world and about how to live. Some people believe the world was created by a God, while others think it arose by chance or else has always existed. Some people think science has given us a picture of the world that is closer to the truth than anything we have had before. Others think that this picture is just the product of a particular culture, and that the 'primitive' world views of other societies are no less correct than ours. Some people think that Marxism is a body of knowledge about history, economics and society, or that psychoanalysis is a body of knowledge about the human mind. Others do not. There are differences about how we should live: about sex, war, abortion, and so on.

When we disagree, this is often because it is difficult to be sure which beliefs are right. But it can also be because of the links between our outlook and our conception of ourselves, between beliefs and our inner story. These links are possible because we have some free play in creating our picture of the world.

Systems of belief
====

A belief is not held in isolation, but is part of a system. Frank Ramsey said that a belief is a 'a map of neighbouring space by which we steer'.[1] Our beliefs about the world hang together, like a mental

---

[1] Frank Ramsey: General Propositions and Causality, in *The Foundations of Mathematics and other Logical Essays*, London, 1931, page 238.

map of a city too large to be fully known. Some parts of the mental map are sharp and detailed, and some hazy. There may be vagueness or mistakes about how some regions join up. And some bits of the map may be inconsistent with others. But, despite these defects, it does not show a series of isolated streets, but a system of streets.

All our beliefs have links to neighbouring ones. I believe that the pills the doctor gives me are likely to help cure the illness I have. This is bound up with my beliefs that he is a good doctor, who goes by recent accounts of the evidence, and that he would not give me a placebo. My expectation about the effectiveness of the medicine is vulnerable to changes in these other beliefs. More generally, if I abandon my present belief in scientific medicine, or my expectation that evidence from the past is a fairly reliable guide to the future, my confidence in the pills will also be undermined. This confidence is bound up with beliefs which in turn are bound up with other parts of my whole network.

There is a simple view, according to which we can decide whether a belief is true or false by comparing it to the bit of the world it corresponds to. But, as many philosophers have pointed out, this is too simple. Suppose the pills do not work. My beliefs obviously need revising. But I have alternative possible responses. I can decide that the doctor is less good than I thought. Or I can postulate some additional factor, perhaps some chemical peculiarity of mine, that interfered with the treatment. Or perhaps the prescribed pills were not prepared properly. At the other extreme, I can give up my good opinion of modern medicine, or even of the scientific methods on which it is based. In the middle range of responses, I can decide that this drug or this illness is less well understood than I had thought.

Some of these responses seem more reasonable than others. And this judgment about reasonableness may in turn be supported or undermined by new information. But the important point is that there are alternative responses to the failure of the medicine. New information, as it comes in, can be interpreted in alternative ways.

This element of free play in interpreting evidence can be exploited by someone determined to cling to a belief. No matter how absurd, any belief *can* be preserved if you are prepared to make sufficient adjustments in the rest of the system. The flat earth can be preserved if you are prepared to postulate a radically different physics, and to explain away satellite pictures as a conspiracy, or as the result of distortions of light in space. A defence of this sort was used against the fossil evidence for evolution: perhaps God, to test our faith, had arranged fossils to look as if evolution had happened.

One model of a system of beliefs is a kind of wire frame sometimes used as a children's toy. The frame is made of many bits of rigid wire. The joints where the bits of wire meet can be adjusted to different angles. You can choose the shape of any bit of the frame, provided you allow the rest of the frame to bend and twist to accommodate it. The belief you want to preserve at all costs is the bit you hold rigid, letting this determine the shape of the rest of the frame. (There does not have to be just one rigid bit. There are degrees of rigidity: a belief may be rigid relative to one part of the system, but flexible relative to others.)

Systems do not only contain beliefs about what the world is like and about what is desirable. Some beliefs are about the plausibility of other ones, and are used to adjudicate between them. They could be called structural beliefs. They are like the load-bearing walls of a house. When a structural belief is given up, there are likely to be changes throughout the rest of the system.

When someone learning science in a school laboratory produces results contradicting a basic law of chemistry, we do not revise our picture of the subject, but explain the results as the product of error. On the other hand, a small number of results by reputable experimenters may be enough to make us abandon a less well-entrenched piece of chemistry. Between these extremes there is a continuum. People along the continuum have very different attitudes towards the amount of evidence needed to establish or refute a hypothesis. Even in science, structural beliefs about plausibility vary from person to person.

This variation is even greater where there is not the underlying consensus likely to exist between two scientists. Suppose one of the scientists is arguing with someone who thinks the whole picture of the world given by physics, chemistry and the biological sciences is just the product of a particular culture, no closer to the truth than the magical views found elsewhere. The defence of the scientific world-view will appeal to the way it is backed by evidence: the theories now accepted are those that have so far best survived the rigours of experimental testing. But the disagreement may be fundamental: why should we accept evidence and experiment as our guides? There is a perhaps worrying circularity. Our reasons for accepting the methods of science are linked to their success. But this success partly consists in producing the picture of the world that is being challenged. Our beliefs about the world interact with our structural beliefs. We accommodate them to each other.

Someone may have a belief, say in Creationism, that conflicts with the evidence. If this belief is a rigid part of their system, the rest can be shaped to fit. But among the beliefs that may need to be reshaped are structural ones. A critic may point out that these revised standards of plausibility, when applied to evidence about other matters, have unwelcome implications. Argument here is largely a matter of spelling out the hidden costs of such a strategy. But people with a really rigid belief in Creationism will be prepared to pay the price. Then we cannot argue with them further.

Beliefs and identity
==

Sometimes beliefs are part of our identity in a quite explicit way. Some people, asked to describe themselves, would make their Catholicism or their Marxism central.

Even people who do not think of themselves mainly in terms of beliefs have lived by them. They have gone to church, consulted the doctor, signed petitions against vivisection, voted, taken up jogging, or had an abortion. Some of the beliefs people act on are unimportant to them. Many people eat brown bread rather than white, because they believe it is better for them. If new evidence suggested that white bread is just as good, adjustment to this would be easy.

But other beliefs have played a more important part. To give them up puts a new interpretation on the past. They may be beliefs you were converted to by someone you loved, so that giving them up seems a repudiation, both of that person and of a high point of your life. Or they may be beliefs you came to at a time of crisis: you feel you drew on the deepest parts of yourself in reaching them. It is especially hard to abandon beliefs for which you have given up a lot: the religious beliefs that led you to spend most of your life as a nun, or the political beliefs for which you were thrown out of a job. Unsurprisingly, these beliefs are often the rigid points of the system.

To abandon them is to rewrite your inner story, perhaps to make it pathetic or a bit ridiculous.

In these ways beliefs can be part of the self we have created. But, as with other aspects of our identity, there are limits to our free play in creating them. We cannot just believe whatever we like. This is because a statement is included among our beliefs only when we think it true. Most of us know that the fact of our wanting to believe something does not make it more likely to be true. Sometimes people deceive themselves, but this requires a special strategy, and is not a matter of just deciding: 'I will now adopt the belief that I am an excellent judge of character.'

We cannot switch on beliefs at will. (Try turning yourself into a holder of the belief that the moon is made of green cheese. Go on: just decide to believe it.) This explains part of what is repulsive about religious doctrines that people are rewarded for belief and punished for unbelief.

This mistake about belief is also what is wrong with Pascal's 'wager'.[2] Pascal argued that religious belief is rational because it is a better bet than unbelief. If believers are wrong, their losses are not great. (Perhaps sex and Sundays have been tinged respectively with guilt and boredom.) But if unbelievers have made the wrong bet, they will spend eternity in hell. Because this is so much worse, belief is the more prudent bet. (And, because hell that never stops is *infinitely* worse, it is rational to bet on belief even where the probability of God existing seems very low.) But, even if persuaded by this argument that it is better to be a believer, I have been given no grounds for *believing*. 'Beliefs' consciously chosen for reasons other than intuitive conviction or grounds for their truth are not really beliefs.

Our inability to believe at will sets limits to self-creation. But we can mould beliefs, using strategies which sometimes come to self-deception. Perhaps what dominates here is the conservative version of self-creation: keeping ourselves as we are. Self-deception is an easier way of maintaining present beliefs than of adopting new ones. This is because the way to retain desired beliefs is to notice and emphasize supporting evidence, and to overlook or discount conflicting evidence. And these tendencies are supported by our views

[2] Blaise Pascal: *Pensées*, translated by A. J. Krailsheimer, Harmondsworth, 1966, Section Two, part two.

about what is plausible, which in turn are linked to the rest of our present system of beliefs.

Consider the way people sometimes protect their beliefs by reading only newspapers they agree with. Take beliefs about crime. In terms of the British press: there is a *Guardian* world, in which crime is caused by unemployment, despite the efforts of underpaid teachers to encourage a sense of responsibility to the community, and despite the efforts of social workers to help families submerged by poverty. There is a *Daily Telegraph* world, where crime results from the decline of moral standards caused by the permissiveness of the 1960s, and where the police are sneered at by so-called 'progressives' whose attitudes have encouraged pornography and the swindling of the taxpayer by scroungers. Someone normally a reader of one of these papers, who one day reads the other, may think some of the stories implausible or untypical, and conclude that the paper presents a biased view. The established set of beliefs is protected from disturbing evidence.

This insulation is a kind of self-deception, often motivated by the way people identify themselves with their political beliefs. But the self-deception grows naturally out of normal rational processes of dealing with evidence. It is rational to be more inclined to believe what sounds plausible. And our structural and other beliefs are inevitably in mutual support.

Some people follow a polite convention that it is best to avoid discussing deep differences of belief, especially about religion or politics. The account sketched here may seem to give reasons for this. Because there is always some free play in our response, no objection to a belief need ever be taken as decisive. So even good arguments may fail to persuade. And, since our sense of what we are like is often bound up with beliefs, criticism of them may seem like an attack on the believer. This gives support to the polite convention.

There are three approaches to disagreement. The first is the most primitive: passionate assertion, together with a defensive anger against those who threaten us by doubting the beliefs we identify with. The second approach, the polite convention, is a natural reaction to this. But to avoid discussion of strongly held beliefs is to shut off a kind of intellectual growth. So some move to a third approach, where discussion is revived, but in a different way.

In this approach, people are again open and explicit about differences of belief. We argue for our own beliefs. We press the other person to explain what we do not understand, and to give reasons for what we doubt. Under this pressure, people's beliefs start to be spelt out in a systematic way, and some basic elements of their system often stand out more clearly. There is a danger of lapsing back into defensive hostility as deeper differences emerge. But the danger is reduced if we look behind the system of possibly mistaken ideas to the person who built it. And to explore the thinking behind a system you deeply disagree with can make it easier to see how its supporters need not be wicked or stupid. (Though their position has problems in the same way yours does.)

Tolstoy, in *Anna Karenina*, has written of one kind of sympathy:

Levin had often noticed in discussions between the most intelligent people that after enormous efforts, and endless logical subtleties and talk, the disputants finally became aware that what they had been at such pains to prove to one another had long ago, from the beginning of the argument, been known to both, but that they liked different things, and would not define what they liked for fear of its being attacked. He had often had the experience of suddenly in the middle of a discussion grasping what it was the other liked and at once liking it too, and immediately he found himself agreeing, and then all arguments fell away useless.[3]

Sympathetic exploration does not always lead to that degree of agreement. Sometimes you can see what the other person likes and find yourself not much liking it. Or else you still care more about something else which conflicts with it. But even where there is persisting disagreement, it is often possible to recognize the intellectual coherence of the other person's views, and at least a bit to see from the inside how they can like what they do like.

The possibility of two people combining intellectual coherence with persisting disagreement brings out something which people often find puzzling about philosophy. On the one hand, philosophy proceeds by rational argument. In philosophy at its best, the arguments are laid out clearly and precisely. So, in principle, the validity of those arguments ought to be objectively checkable, in the way a proof in mathematics is. And yet, on the other hand, philosophers persistently disagree. Asking a group of philosophers whethe-

[3] Leo Tolstoy: *Anna Karenina*, translated by Rosemary Edmonds, Harmondsworth, 1954, page 421.

there is a God, or whether robots could be conscious, is not like asking a group of physiologists about how breathing works.

The apparent lack of clear progress or of a body of established results is an embarrassment to philosophy. It may seem that philosophy is like mathematics, but philosophers are very incompetent, and fail to agree on proofs that should be open to objective decision. Or it may seem that the apparent rigour of the arguments is bogus, a cover for what is really the expression of entirely subjective opinion.

But, while there are incompetent philosophers, and technical complication can be used to give a false impression of rigour, the central explanation is not so damaging. What can be objectively decided is the logical relation between beliefs.

Competent philosophers should be able to agree on the map of what is entailed by holding a particular set of beliefs. Quite often some absurdity is entailed. What can then be objectively established is that, if you want to avoid the absurdity, you must give up certain of the original beliefs. But often there are alternatives about which beliefs to give up, each with their own costs somewhere else. The map leaves a choice about which way to go. And it is always open to someone to accept the 'absurdity' rather than give up any of the beliefs started with.

In philosophy, there are discoveries; there is progress. But the discoveries are about the map, about how beliefs hang together. They do not force you to give up beliefs, though they often show that retaining them has an unsuspectedly high cost. With philosophers, as with other people, the objectivity of logic can, without paradox, coexist with different views of the world.

Discovering and creating beliefs

Discussing differences of belief can be to learn about yourself. We start to see the map of how different beliefs are linked to each other, and we see where our own beliefs fit on the map. Pressed to explain and defend our own views, we discover more of ourselves, by uncovering deeper beliefs we were not aware of before, and by seeing them in contrast with the beliefs of others.

But the process is not just a passive one of becoming aware of something. There is an element of self-creation as well as of self-discovery. Our beliefs come from many sources: our own experience, what we were taught as children, science, religion, what our friends have told us, and from what we have read or have seen on television. A set of beliefs coming from such varied sources almost certainly contains inconsistencies. Both our beliefs about what the world is like, and our set of values, are likely to include contradictions. And, perhaps even more, the structural beliefs needed for one part of the system are likely to be incompatible with those needed for another part.

As discussion reveals these inconsistencies, anyone sufficiently rational to be disturbed by them will have choices to make. Suppose you think that heavier sentences are likely to reduce crime, and I am sceptical about this. I press you for your evidence, and dismiss it as an inadequate mixture of anecdote and intuition about how other people take decisions. But perhaps you remind me that yesterday we were discussing my view that economic sanctions are likely to make the South African government change its policy. You point out the similarity between what I thought was acceptable evidence yesterday and the evidence you have given today. (This is a crude and simple example. Things are rarely as clear-cut as this.) I have a choice between adjusting my view on one issue or on the other.

The choice is partly constrained by the rest of my system of belief. If you show me that the evidence for my beliefs about how to contain inflation is of the same quality that supports belief in witches, it is not open to me simply to decide to believe in witches after all. (When a politician, determined not to lose an argument, makes a move of this kind, we may suspect opportunism and insincerity.) But often I do have a choice of which belief to change, even if my choice is shaped by the need to minimize damage to other parts of my system. And, in making these choices, I go beyond discovering the system to creating it.

Beliefs about beliefs

As we pursue disagreements, we become more aware of the kinds of evidence and reasons that would support beliefs in conflict with ours. And so we become more aware of the ways in which ours are vulnerable. And we also come to see how our beliefs do not simply *follow* from the evidence that supports them, but that they depend on a combination of evidence and structural beliefs. We see how others have different structural beliefs, how ours are linked to other parts of our system, and how they could be challenged.

We also become more self-conscious about weaknesses of our system: about how vague and schematic some bits of the mental map are. As with our inner story, our beliefs about the world involve much abridgment, often of evidence that we have forgotten, or that we were never really on top of. Think of some subject you are not an expert about, such as astronomy or medieval history. Your views are probably inadequately based, too simple, and in some ways mistaken. And yet to have no opinions on such matters would leave huge blanks on the map. We do not like our map of the world to be mainly blank, but the price of this is that much of it is schematic and includes mistakes.

Some people treat their opinions as a religion. They have Beliefs rather than beliefs. (There are not only religious religions, but political, medical and scientific religions as well.) The tendency of critical discussion is to encourage people to move from Belief to belief. Once we see the ways in which our beliefs are vulnerable both to new evidence and to revisions of other parts of the system, it is impossible to revert to the lack of self-consciousness of the simple Believer. We can still identify with our beliefs, but not in the same way. Not only our beliefs themselves, but also our attitudes to them, help to make us what we are. So in this way too, by talking to each other, we change each other and ourselves.

CHAPTER SIXTEEN

===

RECOGNITION

Not universal love
But to be loved alone.

W. H. AUDEN: 'September 1, 1939'.

SELF-CREATION HAS to start
from a picture of what we are like now. We hope that our picture of
our distinctive characteristics is not a private fantasy, but corresponds
to some public reality. For this, it needs to be validated by the
responses of others. We have the inner story of our past. We do not
want it to be a purely private story. Most people do not want to hear
it. (Though some egomaniacs do not notice.) But we hope a few
people will be interested, and will take roughly our view of what we
did. This recognition seems to validate our inner story.

The need for recognition

===

The need for recognition has at least three components. We want
people to see us at least roughly as we think we are. We want to be
respected. And we want to be liked.

The last two needs are linked to the first. To know that you
respect and like me will not be enough if I see that you have an
entirely false picture of me: that you respect me for what you see as
my brilliantly disguised spying activities, or that you like me because
you wrongly think I am your anonymous benefactor.

It has been claimed that denial of recognition in the family can contribute to schizophrenia. Whether or not this is so, denial of recognition certainly frustrates a deeply felt need. The extreme case is refusal to acknowledge someone's existence at all.

William James said,

No more fiendish punishment could be devised, were such a thing physically possible, than that one should be turned loose in society and remain absolutely unnoticed by all the members thereof. If no one turned round when we entered, answered when we spoke, or minded what we did, but if every person we met 'cut us dead', and acted as if we were non-existing things, a kind of rage and impotent despair would ere long well up in us, from which the cruellest bodily tortures would be a relief; for these would make us feel that, however bad might be our plight, we had not sunk to such a depth as to be unworthy of attention at all.[1]

Cases where a non-striking worker has committed suicide, after being 'sent to Coventry' by fellow workers who supported the strike, give some support to James's view.

The desire not to be ignored is only the most basic level of the need for recognition. Some people have a gargantuan appetite for it, wanting to be 'world famous' or to have a reputation that lives on after their death. Even those who do not hope for the lasting fame of a Napoleon or a Newton often hope that what they do will gain at least the respect of some others in their own circle. The pervasiveness of this can be seen in struggles for status: in pay disputes motivated by the relative pay of other groups, in the competition for promotion, honours and prizes. People seem to change physically with public success or defeat: the day after an election, winners and losers look as if quite different chemicals are coursing round inside them. (In a herd of Indian antelope, there is one male leader, marked out by being black. When he dies, his successor turns black. It is thought that the leader emits a pheromone, which stops the others turning black.)

Hegel was the first philosopher to see the importance of other people's recognition. He characteristically projected this psychological insight on to the large screen of world history. Hegel believed that primitive men tried to gain recognition from each other by armed conflict. This was to force others to recognize them. It was also to justify their claim to recognition by their willingness to risk death for it. But the winner in a life-and-death struggle cannot gain recognition from a dead opponent. So there developed the

[1] William James: *The Principles of Psychology*, New York, 1890, volume 1, page 293.

more satisfactory alternative of enslaving rather than killing the defeated rival. But the forced recognition of the master by the slave is unsatisfactorily one-sided: 'What now confronts him is not an independent consciousness but a dependent one.' So the slave cannot give the kind of recognition hoped for. The dictator whose trembling subordinates write eulogistic reviews of his books of 'thoughts' is making the same mistake as the lonely person who pays other people to send him Christmas cards. God must have the same problem.

Recognition needs others, who are independent and who are willing to give it. But it also needs circumstances allowing the growth of features for them to recognize. Some social institutions stifle people by a regimentation designed to suppress individual differences, so that recognition is minimized, and the will to independent action may become atrophied. But the renewal of recognition can bring it alive again. Perhaps the greatest depersonalization of this kind took place in the Nazi concentration camps. Bruno Bettelheim discusses this in the light of an extraordinary case of defiance of the process:

Once, a group of naked prisoners about to enter the gas chamber stood lined up in front of it. In some way the commanding SS officer learned that one of the women prisoners had been a dancer. So he ordered her to dance for him. She did, and as she danced, she approached him, seized his gun, and shot him down. She too was immediately shot to death.

But isn't it probable that despite the grotesque setting in which she danced, dancing made her once again a person? Dancing, she was singled out as an individual, asked to perform in what had once been her chosen vocation. No longer was she a number, a nameless, depersonalized prisoner, but the dancer she used to be. Transformed, however momentarily, she responded like her old self, destroying the enemy bent on her destruction, even if she had to die in the process. [2]

Relationships

Recognition is often impersonal. Film stars, footballers, politicians and singers are given recognition by people they do not know. Those who want fame and reputation hope for this impersonal response. But people also need a different recognition, that comes with individual contact.

[2] Bruno Bettelheim: *The Informed Heart*, London, 1970, pages 239–240.

Impersonal recognition perhaps gives the most objective picture of someone, through being detached from the bias of a single person's perspective. But personal recognition, if more subjective, may give a deeper picture, drawing on things not publicly available. People vary in the kind of recognition they care about. A national leader may care more about the verdict of history than about the verdict of her husband and friends. But, for most ordinary people, it is different. Only a rather self-important person, after quarrelling with his wife, would leave the verdict to history.

Most of us want a recognition whose value depends on relationships and which helps us make them. Of course recognition is only part of what we look for in a relationship. A larger part is the pleasure we take in the distinctive qualities of the other person. Only narcissists are *mainly* interested in other people as a mirror.

Forming close relationships depends on qualities people have. We pass thousands of people in life without making real contact. But there is mutual recognition when we meet people of our own kind. It can come from similar responses or a shared sense of humour. (This is like the selective adhesiveness of different types of cells during the development of the embryo. Cells of one organ, such as the liver, will bond with other liver cells but not with kidney cells.)

Aristotle said, 'Without friends no one would choose to live, though he had all other goods.'[3] Even leaving aside sex, relationships meet strong emotional needs. We value the things we do and the experiences we have: if we did not we might as well be unconscious or dead. But we also mind that we have someone to share them with. To be on your own, for an experience that seems to matter, can be to regret that no one is sharing it. A spectacular sunset seen alone can give a feeling of incompleteness. But it is not enough simply that other people are having the same experience: to know, as you look at the sunset, that the hillside is dotted with strangers, out of earshot of each other, also seeing it. The need is for mutual awareness in sharing the experience. I am aware of the sunset, of your response to it, of your awareness of my awareness of all this, and so on. And, because I know you, I know more about your response than a stranger would.

[3] Aristotle: *Nicomachean Ethics*, translated by Sir David Ross, Oxford, 1925, Book 8.

If someone feels lonely, and goes on his own to the cinema, these levels of mutual recognition will not be there. However large the audience, he will not have the kind of shared experience that would end his loneliness.

What is recognized in relationships need not be already complete. The qualities recognized may be partly drawn out in relationships and partly created by them. When selective adhesiveness takes place, the relationship often draws on deeper levels of us which would otherwise be unexpressed. When we talk to each other, we draw out reactions and thoughts which only exist fully when expressed. In this way, as well as by absorbing each other's responses, we share in creating each other's inner story. Sometimes, almost unconsciously, we do things with another person as the half-intended audience. If the other person dies, this becomes clear when you notice that they are not there to see or be told.

Commitments

Derek Parfit suggests that the abandonment of the ego, and the transition from identity to survival, weaken the force of commitments.[4] Survival is a matter of degree, and past selves may fade over time. Perhaps a promise made by my past self to your past self gives your present self at best a reduced claim on me now. The boundaries between people become less important, and the differences between successive selves become more so.

Seeing the boundaries between people as less important would have a problematic effect on relationships. Part of loving someone is an intense interest in what she is like, together with an awareness of her response to you. It matters that you are with her. If she cannot come, it is not almost as good if she sends her sister or her aunt instead. The boundary between the person you love and other people cannot seem relatively unimportant.

The boundary between her present self and other people is important because she is different from other people in her characteristics. But, if we took the more radical view, the boundary between her present self and her later selves would be just as

[4] Derek Parfit: *Reasons and Persons*, Oxford, 1984, pages 326–329.

important. To take this view would make long-term commitment impossible. And this would make it impossible to give yourself fully now. You would always be aware that you were only loaning yourself until she changed or until you did.

There is also something disturbing about applying to someone you love the line of thought which is supposed to make death less bad. If, instead of saying, 'She will be dead,' I say, 'There will be no future experiences psychologically connected to her present experiences,' I do not find this cheers me up at all. It will not be nearly as good if similar experiences will still occur, though located somewhere else.

The undercutting of relationships would be a disaster. But, if people did fade fast, the disaster would be unavoidable once we saw things clearly. But there are two reasons for thinking people do not fade so fast. One is that many of the features that contribute to a person's distinctiveness (such as likes and dislikes, or style) seem usually fairly stable. The other is the importance of the inner story which spans our lives. Through mutual recognition, we can share the creation of our inner story with others. So we can change in partly interlocking ways, and avoid the disaster of our commitments and relationships fading away.

CHAPTER SEVENTEEN

THE SOCIAL SELF

ONE OBJECTION TO the possibility of self-creation takes up the idea that other people shape us. We know they do this. There are the platitudes of child psychology about the influence of family and friends. There is the more interesting, though more controversial, evidence of the severe sensory, intellectual and emotional limitations of 'wolf children', who have spent their early childhood without human contact. But, to most of us, the extent to which we are influenced by others, and not just in childhood, is apparent without need for scientific study.

There is the view that our identity is constructed by society. Two variants of this approach are worth distinguishing. The first, a version of what is known as role theory, says that the idea of an inner core of a person is an illusion. The inner core can be analysed without remainder into the playing of various social roles. (This account is something of an idealization. Perhaps no one holds the view in quite this stark form, but the idealized version exercises a pull, even if it is rarely fully adopted.) The second, more sophisticated, variant accepts that people have an inner core which transcends the roles they play, but says the inner core is itself a social construct. I shall consider the role analysis first, and then the more subtle variant.

Role theory

The price we pay for belonging to society is conforming to people's expectations. Doctors dress like this; waiters move like that; singers do not have the same hairstyles as nurses or bank managers; this is how parents talk to their children; clergymen do not tell jokes like that. The pressure can come from a job demanding a deference that is not felt, or from expectations perhaps associated with stereotyped sex roles. Sometimes the required conformity seems alien to us, though we often get used to it and no longer mind. But perhaps this is a deeper conformity.

It can seem that each of us could be analysed without remainder into the various long or short term social roles we play. On this view, what I do is a function of what is expected of someone who is married, a parent, male, white, English, a university lecturer, in his forties, part of a queue waiting for a bus, and so on. Items on this list explain why I am dressed as I am, rather than wearing a cowboy hat, or a dress. They explain why I am not pushing and shoving to the front of the queue. They explain why, instead of entertaining the other people with snatches of song and dance, I am standing at the back, quietly putting up with the rain.

And, this line of thought goes on, as you extend the list of social positions I occupy, together with the corresponding expectations, everything I do can be explained in the same way. We may seem to be trapped. We want relationships that are personal, where we respond to each other's particular characteristics, and where it is not just as good if someone else is here instead. Relationships require society. But, on this view, social life obliterates anything distinctively ours to be recognized.

We are all familiar with the way pressures to conform are tied to categories that create social roles: to your job, your gender, your age and so on. These pressures can force people into patterns they find alien. And over time a false self can grow into a genuine one. People in prison can become institutionalized, coming to feel more at home there than outside. (My children once felt sorry for a pony, permanently tethered to a stick so that he could only walk in a circle round it. They untied him, but he went on walking round the circle.)

One feature of role theory is how hard it is to escape from. It is natural to think that some of the time we are acting out social roles, but that at other times we are able just to relax and be ourselves. (Perhaps there are evenings when the Pope is sitting in his pyjamas with a glass of cherry brandy, watching a Hitchcock film on television.) But sociologists have applied role analysis even to the informal parts of life.

Erving Goffman argued that the things we do which seem to escape from social roles are themselves refinements of those roles. A surgeon who jokes with the nurses before an operation may be sending a signal that he is not just a surgeon, but is human too. These ways in which we distance ourselves from role behaviour are themselves subject to analysis. The signal that we are not taking something quite seriously has itself to be understood, and so it too will have an element of convention in it. Goffman described the way we see this distancing from roles:

There is a vulgar tendency in social thought to divide the conduct of the individual into a profane and sacred part ... The profane part is attributed to the obligatory world of social roles; it is formal, stiff, and dead; it is exacted by society. The sacred part has to do with 'personal' matters and 'personal' relationships – with what an individual is 'really' like underneath it all when he relaxes and breaks through to those in his presence. It is here, in this personal capacity, that an individual can be warm, spontaneous, and touched by humour. It is here, regardless of his social role, that an individual can show 'what kind of a guy he is'.[1]

Goffman described this as a 'touching tendency to keep a part of the world safe from sociology'. He argued against it on the grounds that personal style is displayed in role distance, which is 'almost as much subject to role analysis as the core tasks of roles themselves'. If he is right, much even of what we take to be the inner core of a person seems to be a social product.

Doubts about role theory

Role theory is supported by the way people seem to behave inconsistently in different contexts. This casts doubt on their having a stable inner core. One problem with this claim is that apparently inconsistent actions may reflect a character that is consistent but complex.

Proust describes an incident in which his narrator's family, coming back from church, met their neighbour, M. Legrandin, walking with a woman. Legrandin astonished them by barely acknowledging their greeting, as though he hardly recognized them. Later Legrandin behaved with his normal friendliness. Proust comments:

[1] Erving Goffman: Role Distance, in *Where the Action Is*, London, 1969, page 103.

It was like every attitude or action which reveals a man's underlying character; they bear no relation to what he has previously said, and we cannot confirm our suspicions by the culprit's own testimony, for he will admit nothing; we are reduced to the evidence of our senses, and we ask ourselves, in the face of this detached and incoherent fragment of recollection, whether indeed our senses have not been the victims of a hallucination . . .[2]

Legrandin's disdainful response seemed out of character. We do not have to interpret it as showing that he did not have stable character traits. Various interpretations are possible, one being Proust's, that it revealed a hidden side of his character. His motives for not introducing Proust's family to his companion could well be a persisting part of a character more complex than they had previously realized.

Another doubt is whether the role pressures on us are really too great to allow any distinctively personal characteristics. Imagine a community organized with the overriding goal of obliterating people's sense of their own individuality. In this society, no activities are allowed except the standard role-bearing ones, such as serving the food and sweeping the floor. There is no talking except to utter the standardized words of roles: 'Please give me the broom for sweeping the floor.' Communication by smiles or other facial expressions, gestures, or eye contact is forbidden. People of both sexes wear the same uniform clothes, and all heads are shaved. Everyone has to answer to a number, not a name. There are no customs where particular people or particular kinds of people perform certain tasks: everyone takes a turn at all of them. And there is no possibility of pride in how you do a job. Any unusual 'improvements' are messed up as they are made.

In such circumstances, some sense of individuality might be preserved by 'internal emigration': the inner life of thought might be the last refuge of the self. But even this might be largely obliterated by some mental version of a treadmill, such as constant pressure to call out answers to problems in mental arithmetic.

Regimentation is not the only way of squeezing self-creation. Those who have been tortured, terrified or starved know how consciousness can be pared down to a single desperate concern. David Piper described this effect of the hunger he and others experienced in Japanese camps in the Second World War:

[2] Marcel Proust: *Remembrance of Things Past*, translated by C. K. Scott Moncrieff and Terence Kilmartin, London, 1981, volume 1, pages 137–8.

Acute hunger, stretched over years, is beyond the normal scope of Europeans and Americans. In practice, it becomes quite quickly paramount; it strips the body to a bleak anatomy, and dissolves mind and spirit within one ravenous physical appetite. Below a certain subsistence level, other considerations vanish – for three and a half years, for example, the needs of sex were nil. On the other hand, the urgency of hunger was the essential governor of survival, its insistent concentration surely the reason why so few prisoners went mad ... In the camps it could seem as if, when it came to the crunch, the ultimate, the only essential quality of man was animal hunger; all other qualities were but fatty accretions, inessential and permissible only in certain artificially contrived conditions of civilization; all luxuries, and the idea of a soul a belch, after the rice issue had been unexpectedly large.[3]

These cases of extreme pressure bring out the exaggerations of role theory. Those of us who are not starving have opportunities for self-creation denied to those who are. And one of the many ways in which ordinary life is unlike a concentration camp is that most of the expected kinds of behaviour are not literally enforced. We are all constrained by social roles and subject to social pressures. But there are degrees of pressure, and only irresistible pressure would leave us no chance to develop a central core of resisting individuality.

Perhaps some people have wanted to keep sociology from studying the more personal parts of life, and perhaps this is a mistake. But rejecting this need not involve giving up the rest of the 'vulgar tendency in social thought'. For there is a contrast between the formal, stiff and dead roles demanded by convention and our embellishments on them. These embellishments add up to a personal style. No doubt style is expressed by means of conventions that can be analysed. But this does not make it less personal. We have to use rule-governed language in talking to each other, but what we say can still be distinctively ours.

Of course we are shaped by people's expectations of us, and of course these vary with our job, our sex, our age, and so on. But it is an illusion to think that we are utterly malleable, submitting entirely to social moulding. This picture might fit people who had no inner story. They would have no conception of themselves apart from the conception other people had. They would lack desires and values in the light of which to criticize the demands made of them, and would

[3] David Piper: I am Well, Who are you?, *The Observer Magazine*, 1968, reprinted in Myra Barrs (ed.): *Identity*, Harmondsworth, 1973.

have no independent views about how their story should continue. We are not such people.

The social construction of the inner core

==

We have an inner core that enables us to bring something distinctive to the roles we play. To develop the 'role' metaphor, we are more like real actors than like the stereotyped characters of a cartoon film. And we are actors who can improvise a lot of the script as we go, and can often choose to walk out and act in a different play.

The more subtle and plausible version of the view that identity is socially constructed accepts all this, but says that the inner core is itself a social product. This is less threatening, as it attempts to explain, rather than undermine, our uniqueness. And this version would only be a threat to the possibility of self-creation if the way society constructs our inner core has to bypass any decisions and choices of ours.

Part of the case for the social construction of the inner core appeals to the social nature of language. What we are is influenced by how we think of ourselves. But we do not think of ourselves according to a private conceptual scheme of our own. We use the concepts of the language we have learnt, and that language is the product of a particular society.

This case raises some disputed issues in philosophy: whether there can be concepts and categories private to a particular person, and whether some concepts and categories are unavoidable features of thought, and so must transcend a particular society. But, whatever the answers to these questions, it is surely plausible that societies show conceptual variations and that our thinking, at least in part, is shaped by the categories of our own society. This would only be worrying if the use of a pre-existing language excluded thinking anything original or distinctive, which clearly it does not.

Part of the social constructionist case is more directly relevant to self-creation. It is based on the role played by other people in the way we form a picture of ourselves.

Knowing what I am like
===

Our conception of our physical size depends on comparison with other physical objects. (Imagine yourself the only thing in empty space, trying to decide how big you are.) Our picture of our personal characteristics depends in a similar way on contrasts with other people. If Robinson Crusoe lived on his island (without Man Friday) so long that he had only hazy memories of other people, he would find it hard to separate his own distinctive features from common human characteristics.

Partly we get to know ourselves by direct comparison with others: compared to me, he can run faster, she is quicker to grasp a point, and they are both more assertive in conversation. But a lot of the self-knowledge we get from others does not come from direct comparison. It comes from awareness of their responses to us. The image of other people's eyes as a mirror expresses part of this. The other person's eyes, facial expression, tone of voice, posture, gestures, and choice of words are all part of a continuous corrective feedback about the impression we are making.

G. H. Mead suggested that this feedback, combined with our ability to imagine things from someone else's perspective, is the basis of our sense of self. He said that children move from play, in which they act out a particular role, to rule-governed games with several participants. On making this move, they have to see their actions from the perspective of what Mead calls the 'Generalized Other': that of all the other players at once, rather than from the viewpoint of another single person. Mead thought that our sense of our own identity is in this way a social construct, based on our ability to imagine ourselves from this impersonal social perspective.[4]

Perhaps some theory of this kind is true. Though feedback about ourselves is directly corrective only if we care about the responses of others. (The sergeant may be well aware of the unfavourable impression the recruits are forming of him.) But, a lot of the time, most of us do care about others having a favourable, or at least an accurate, impression of us, and so the feedback influences what we do.

[4] G. H. Mead: *Mind, Self, and Society from the Standpoint of a Social Behaviorist*, Chicago, 1934, Part Three.

Some oblivious people notably do not have this feedback, which can result in them gently drifting away from others. Awareness, with a willingness to make some corrective adjustments, helps to keep us sufficiently alike for easy relationships. We do not value total conventionality. But below a certain level of mutual adjustment we find it harder to get on with each other. This is sometimes seen when groups of people have been separated for a long time. Biologists have the concept of genetic drift, where a small sub-group of a population, left to breed on its own, ends up with different gene frequencies from that of the parent population. A similar process of 'cultural drift' can be seen where groups of people are cut off in small communities with little or no communication with their parent group.

Our characteristics are often influenced by our beliefs about them. If I think I am awkward or clumsy, this belief may make me more so. So feedback from others about my awkwardness, by reinforcing my belief, may reinforce the awkwardness too.

Manipulating the feedback from others is a powerful way of changing how someone sees himself. This comes out in descriptions of the 'Thought Reform' carried out on political prisoners in China soon after the Revolution. Robert Jay Lifton described the process:

From the beginning, Dr Vincent was told he was not really a doctor, that all of what he considered himself to be was merely a cloak under which he hid what he really was. And Father Luca was told the same thing, especially about the area he held most precious – his religion. Backing up this assertion were all of the physical and emotional assaults of early imprisonment ... Dr Vincent and Father Luca each began to lose his bearings on who and what he was, and where he stood in relationship to his fellows. Each felt his sense of self become amorphous and impotent and fall more and more under the control of its would-be remoulders.[5]

Lifton quotes one of them describing this process:

'You have the feeling that you look to yourself on the people's side and that you are a criminal. Not all of the time – but moments – you think they are right. "I did this, I am a criminal." If you doubt, you keep it to yourself. Because if you admit the doubt you will be "struggled" and lose the progress you have made ... In this way they built up a spy mentality ... They built up a criminal ... Then your invention becomes a reality ... You feel guilty, because all of the time you have to look at yourself from the people's standpoint ...'[6]

[5] Robert Jay Lifton: *Thought Reform and the Psychology of Totalism*, Harmondsworth, 1967, page 86.
[6] Ibid., page 43.

Such cases are obviously extreme. But the effectiveness of manipulating feedback in this way (admittedly combined with other pressures) fits in with the view that 'Thought Reform' made use of the normal need for recognition, and of our resulting responsiveness to the picture others have of us. This responsiveness is one of the mechanisms by which, in ordinary life, we do not just gain self-knowledge from others, but are moulded by them as well.

The inner core and determinism

What we do is not simply predictable from the social pressures now brought to bear on us. To decisions we bring our own beliefs, values and conception of ourselves. To relationships and to our work, we bring a feeling for what is really us: an awareness of flourishing or of being stifled.

But this inner core does not come from nowhere. There are good reasons for thinking that it has in turn been shaped by such things as the categories of our language and the responses of others to what we have done. This does not exclude self-creation, which bases decisions about what I shall be like on this inner core. Also, none of this demonstrates that the inner core is entirely created by society. There is the alternative view that it results from interaction between earlier social influences and my genetic make-up. It is an empirical question what contribution these different factors make.

Self-creation requires that I can shape myself in the light of my commitments and desires. Whether this is possible does not depend on their causal origin. On the other hand, there is the view that causal determinism rules out the freedom of choice needed for self-creation. If this is right, self-creation is impossible, whether the causal factors are hereditary or environmental.

CHAPTER EIGHTEEN

===

IS SELF-CREATION POSSIBLE?

SELF-CREATION CAN seem impossible. There are two main reasons for this. First, it has an air of logical paradox. From eggs come chickens who lay eggs from which other chickens come. Yet we do not expect a chicken to create itself by laying its own egg. Obviously *complete* self-creation would be equally paradoxical. But I hope the impression of paradox has been weakened. Self-creation can be at best partial. We have to start with values, desires and other characteristics which we do not ourselves create. The other reason for thinking self-creation impossible is based on a determinist view of the world.

What we do is not simply a function of the various social pressures on us. Those pressures interact with desires, plans, projects and values that are distinctively ours. In exactly the same circumstances you and I may act differently. All this is small comfort to someone whose scepticism is based on a more general determinism. What I do is caused, not by social circumstances alone, but by their interplay with characteristics that are distinctively mine. Yet where do these characteristics of mine come from? They are produced by my genes interacting with the environment I have had.

Some of the environmental influences on us have already been mentioned. There is also evidence that people's genetic differences contribute to the different ways they behave. Until recently, this was based mainly on twin studies. The degree of psychological similarity of identical twins was compared to that of fraternal twins. Or twins reared separately in different environments were compared. The passionate battles between those who 'know' that we are mainly the product of our genes and those who 'know' that environmental causes are dominant have been mainly about how these studies should be interpreted.

Whatever the truth about the relative contributions of genes and environment to particular characteristics, some of the most intuitively striking support for the view that there *is* a role for genes is anecdotal. In a number of cases of twins separated at birth, what was striking when they met for the first time as adults was not so much a general similarity of temperament, but the way small quirks would turn out to be the same. Sometimes they would have given their children the same names, or both would have built a white seat round a tree in the garden, or both would obsessively count the wheels on passing lorries, or both would be afraid of the sea and would go into it carefully backwards, or both would have a habit of pushing up their noses (which both would call 'squidging').[1] These cases, if not coincidental, suggest that genetic influences on behaviour can be surprisingly localized and specific.

Support of a different kind for a genetic influence on some kinds of behaviour comes from neurochemistry. The causal mechanisms by which genes influence behaviour are now starting to be worked out. There is a pattern of behaviour that makes psychiatrists classify someone as 'sensation-seeking'. It manifests itself in an unusually strong disposition towards activities ranging from gambling to parachute jumping, and is correlated with such psychiatric problems as alcoholism. In repeated studies, sensation-seeking has been found to be correlated with low levels of activity of platelet monoamine oxidase.[2] This level in turn has been shown by twin studies to be largely under genetic control.[3]

Evidence of this sort enables us to start tracing out the pathways by which genes influence our chemistry, which in turn influences our behaviour. When combined with evidence of the effectiveness of environmental influences, it sketches, in rough and very incomplete outline, a determinist picture of human beings.

In such a picture, our actions can all be explained in terms of (no

---

[1] Peter Watson: *Twins*, London, 1981.
[2] Monte S. Buchsbaum, Robert D. Coursey and Dennis L. Murphy: The Biochemical High-Risk Paradigm: Behavioural and Familial Correlates of Low Platelet Monoamine Oxidase Activity, *Science*, 1976; Lars von Knorring, Lars Oreland and Bengt Winblad: Personality Traits Related to Monoamine Oxidase Activity in Platelets, *Psychiatry Research*, 1984.
[3] Alexander Nies, Donald S. Robinson, Kathleen R. Lamborn and Richard P. Lampert: Genetic Control of Platelet and Plasma Monoamine Oxidase Activity, *Archives of General Psychiatry*, 1973; Michael A. Revely, Adrianne M. Revely, Christine A. Clifford and Robin M. Murray: Genetics of Platelet MAO Activity in Discordant Schizophrenic and Normal Twins, *British Journal of Psychiatry*, 1983.

doubt very complicated) causal mechanisms. If this model is right, it seems that what we do, just as much as what billiard balls do, is the product of a set of causal laws operating in particular circumstances. This determinist picture seems to undermine the possibility of self-creation. Does it?

Determinism

On the most general version of determinism, all events, including human actions, are the product of causal laws.

Determinists sometimes exempt events at the sub-atomic level, which in the view of many physicists do not display causal regularities. We can accept that determinism does not hold at the sub-atomic level, without thinking this makes any difference to determinism at the level of human behaviour. Perhaps the causal laws relevant to predicting human behaviour have to do with brain mechanisms. Statistical regularities at the level of sub-atomic events are enough to allow predictability at the level of nerve impulses crossing synapses.

The determinist picture seems disturbing. It suggests that a God-like scientist, with complete knowledge of all the relevant causal laws, and of the circumstances in which they operated, could successfully predict any human action. If anyone did anything other than the predicted action, this would falsify one or more of the causal laws. But, the argument goes, determinism requires that some set of relevant causal laws is true, and this is incompatible with their being falsified. So determinism is incompatible with anyone not doing the predicted action. Ruling out all courses of action but one, it seems incompatible with genuine choice.

In two different ways determinism is at least an apparent threat to self-creation. First, the elimination of genuine choice would leave no room for choosing what sort of person to be. The second threat is more oblique. Undermining choice seems also to undermine many of our emotional reactions to people. The determinist picture may not leave room for justifiable resentment of what people do, or for justifiable feelings of blame or guilt. These attitudes play a part in self-creation, and seem threatened by determinism.

The simplest, but least satisfactory, reply to this line of thought is to say that determinism is untrue, or at least that we do not know it is true.

What matters is whether determinism is true, not whether we know it is. If it is true, our ignorance does not neutralize any threat, but just keeps us from seeing that we need to worry.

Rejecting determinism is an unsatisfactory way of escape. It is hard to see how we could prove that at, say, the neurophysiological level, there must be some events that cannot be causally explained. There are of course many neurophysiological events we cannot now explain. But we cannot rule out causal explanations as yet undiscovered. And, even if there were uncaused events in the brain, there seems no reason to suppose that they would play a part in decisions. Finally, there is the problem of how gaps in the causal process, even if they did occur at the point of decision, would make actions free. The objection is sometimes made that causal gaps only add an element of randomness. How could this be the basis of a free decision?

For these reasons, alternatives to the determinist account will not be explored here. It will be assumed that any plausible view will not depend on gaps in the causal story.

On this assumption, we are left with the choice between what William James once called 'hard' and 'soft' determinism. Hard determinism is the disturbing line of thought we are considering: the view that determinism rules out genuine choice, and so also rules out the emotional responses linked with holding people responsible for what they do. Soft determinism asserts that free choice and responsibility are compatible with determinism. (In some versions, they even require it.) Soft determinism (sometimes known as 'compatibilism') assumes, just as much as hard determinism (sometimes known as 'incompatibilism'), that in principle actions are completely predictable. It is not 'soft' because of any fuzziness in the causal laws.

The issue is whether the soft determinist can resist the hard determinist argument against freedom and the reactive attitudes. Soft determinists have developed three main alternative strategies for doing this. The first strategy points out that determinism is not the same as fatalism: that, even in a determinist world, what we do influences the future. The second challenges the claim that determinism eliminates genuine choice. The aim is to work out a model of free action that is compatible with determinism. The third strategy, rejecting a later stage of the hard determinist argument, is to defend responsibility, and the responses associated with it, in ways that sidestep issues about alternative possibilities of choice.

The rejection of fatalism
==

A fatalist thinks that there is no point in my doing anything, as the future will be as it will be, regardless of what I do. This is a silly view, whether or not determinism is true. It has the consequence that I may as well drive when drunk, since, if there is going to be an accident, nothing I decide can make the slightest difference. In a determinist world, outcomes are the result of earlier causes, and there is no reason why my decisions and actions should be excluded from those causes.

Models of free action
==

Our decisions play a role in the causal process. This is part of the defence of the possibility of self-creation. Our own character is one of the things to which our decisions can make a difference. But this defence, valid as far as it goes, leaves deeper issues untouched. Our decisions make a difference. But, in a determinist world, are not our decisions themselves outside our control?

We have seen the central role of beliefs and desires in our everyday explanations. Adding one more component, we can see actions as the product of beliefs, desires and abilities. Consider some ways in which I may fail to do something expected of me. Perhaps I have agreed to meet you, but I do not turn up. The failure may result from my beliefs: I misremembered the day. Or it may reflect my desires: I wanted to do something else more. Or it may result from lack of ability: I tried to come, but on the way I fell and broke my leg.

In our everyday thinking about such episodes, defects of abilities and beliefs are seen as possible limitations on freedom. Not having the right set of desires is not usually thought of as any kind of lack of freedom. This is reflected in the kinds of excuse we accept. You will not blame me when I was not able to come because of the broken leg. And blame may be at least reduced where I meant to come but was wrong about the day. But the fact that I preferred to do something else is not even a candidate for being an excuse.

Accounts of free action differ in the kinds of defects of beliefs and abilities that are seen as impairing freedom. Here I shall ignore beliefs, and concentrate on abilities. The simplest accounts of how freedom is limited by lack of ability focus on very obvious external factors. My freedom to act is reduced if I am locked up or threatened by a gun. But not all limitations of a person's ability are external. The most obvious 'internal' defects involve lack of physical ability: I was not strong enough to force open the door.

The hard determinist argument often relies on the words 'can' and 'could'. It says that, if what I do is predictable on the basis of causal laws, then I cannot avoid doing it. If what I did yesterday was predictable in the same way, I could not have done otherwise. Determinism seems to entail that I cannot do anything except the things I do. Soft determinists, challenging the argument, have objected to this step. The objection appeals to how we ordinarily think about abilities: what we mean when we say that we can or cannot do things. The objection is that there is a perfectly good sense of 'can' in which I can do many things I do not do. And, similarly, there is a perfectly good sense of 'could' in which I could have done many things I did not do.

A classic statement of this objection was by G. E. Moore. He said, 'I *could* have walked a mile in twenty minutes this morning, but I certainly could *not* have run two miles in five minutes,' and 'It is true, as a rule, that cats *can* climb trees, whereas dogs can't.'[4] (I like 'as a rule'. No one is going to catch out Moore by citing some cat with amputated legs.)

On Moore's view, I can do something if nothing will frustrate my choice to do it. This fits well with one of our main reasons for being interested in what people can and cannot do. Where I do not keep our appointment, you may be interested in whether this was because I was unable to or because I did not want to. If I did not want to,

4 G. E. Moore: *Ethics*, Oxford, 1912, chapter 6.

you will see this as indicating an unsatisfactory or blameworthy attitude. But, if I was unable to meet you, criticism of my attitude does not arise. People's motives and attitudes are central to our relationships with them, in a way their abilities usually are not. And Moore's test, of whether there were factors that would frustrate a decision to act in the desirable way, is obviously relevant to seeing whether failure stems from attitude or lack of ability.

This case for soft determinism starts with an account of what it is to be able to do something. I am able to walk a mile in twenty minutes, in that nothing would frustrate any decision to do so. And I have this ability even if I do not choose to use it. None of this is upset by the truth of determinism. And the presence of such abilities is all that is presupposed when we hold people responsible for what they do.

But this is at best only a first stage in constructing an adequate soft determinist account of free action. Suppose there is a sense of 'can' or 'could' which is to be explained along the lines Moore suggests. Perhaps there is also another sense in which 'he could have done otherwise' is excluded by determinism. (It is the sense in which, given the laws of physics and the forces bearing on them, billiard balls cannot move anywhere except where they do.) Do we know that this other sense can be ignored when we are thinking about someone's freedom to act?

The importance we attach to motive and attitude suggests that Moore's sense of 'can' is central to our present practice of holding people responsible. The hard determinist may accept this. But he may go on to say that, because (in the other sense) we cannot do anything except what we do, our present practices are indefensible. And this case cannot be answered simply by saying what our present practices are.

There is another doubt about this version of soft determinism. It makes a sharp separation between desires and abilities. This may not be a problem when we are concerned with physical abilities. But, with psychological abilities, the separation seems less clear. Consider possible causes of 'diminished responsibility', such as alcoholism or compulsive desires to steal. In these cases, there may be other blocks to freedom, as well as those which come between choice and action. Perhaps choices themselves can be unfree. And, even apart from these special cases, it is reasonable to ask, 'I can do what I choose, but can I choose what I choose?' Or, as the question is sometimes put, 'I can do what I want, but can I want what I want?'

In reply to this, a more sophisticated soft determinist account overlaps with some of the things that have been said about self-creation. We do not just have desires to act, but higher-order attitudes towards those desires. There are second-order desires: someone can want not to have his desire to smoke.

Harry Frankfurt has developed an account in which these points are central.[5] Frankfurt calls the first-order desire that is expressed in choice the person's 'will'. He says that freedom of action is being able to do what you want. (It is what Moore was concerned with.) But, for Frankfurt, there is also freedom of will: the ability to have the will you want. He thinks that these two freedoms together make up the whole of freedom. He says of someone who has both: 'Then he is not only free to do what he wants to do; he is also free to want what he wants to want. It seems to me that he has, in that case, all the freedom it is possible to desire or to conceive.'

There is a problem for this sophisticated account of freedom of will, parallel to the problem faced by Moore's one-level account of freedom of action. At whatever level of desire we stop, can we not ask whether *that* desire was avoidable? There seems a danger of having to go endlessly further back, asking whether someone desires to desire to desire to act, and so on. Frankfurt replies that when someone decisively identifies with a desire, wanting without reservation or conflict to act on it, this blocks any further questions.

This is an attractive account of freedom. It rightly includes Moore's requirement that I must not be prevented from implementing my decisions. But it also rightly adds a further condition, that I must endorse without reservation the desires that prevail in my actions. This allows us to explain why the reluctant addict, who satisfies his craving, is not free. Perhaps when Frankfurt's two conditions are met, I have 'all the freedom it is possible to desire or to conceive'. But, even so there remains the question of whether I have enough to justify people holding me responsible.

Take someone who, with the highest degree of freedom, makes a living out of forging banknotes. If he had decided not to make forgeries, he would have implemented that decision. And he feels no conflict. He does not wish he could give up forgery: he feels no moral scruples, and is happy to think of himself as a forger. He seems the ideal candidate for blame.

When we express our blame, he has a reply. (He is a forger with a degree in philosophy. He has read this book, which he stole from a friend, and also Frankfurt's article, which he ripped out of a volume in a library.) His reply concedes that we can shape ourselves in the light of our attitudes and values. And desires can be influenced by higher-order desires. But all this has to start with some set of attitudes and desires that we just take as given. And the content of the set we start with is the product of our genes and early environment, neither of which we could choose. What we start with is just good or bad luck. And surely it is unfair to blame people for the results of their luck in the genetic and environmental lotteries.

The debate about free action is inconclusive. The soft determinist produces increasingly sophisticated refinements in his model, but he is unable to purge it of all elements of luck. He says the element of luck is unimportant: it is absurd to suppose that responsibility requires more freedom than we can desire or conceive. The hard determinist is unimpressed, agreeing with the forger's point about the unfairness of blame for what depends on luck. It is not clear what more can be said about free action on either side, and the argument seems to end in stalemate.

Defences of the reactive attitudes
==

The alternative soft determinist strategy is to give a direct defence of reactive attitudes to people. The claim is that praise and blame, pride and guilt, gratitude and resentment, can be justified, regardless of whether, at the deepest level, our actions are free.

A simple version of this strategy was used by Moritz Schlick to defend praise and blame.[6] He stressed the social usefulness of these responses. Praise and blame, like reward and punishment, can be used to manipulate people, giving them motives to change their behaviour.

No doubt social pressures often function through our desire to be

[6] Moritz Schlick: *Problems of Ethics*, translated by David Rynin, New York, 1939, chapter 7.

praised or to avoid blame. But consciously setting out to manipulate people by means of praise and blame is not straightforward. Blame influences people in two different ways. It can operate by surface pressure: people do not like being spoken to sharply, or being treated in an unfriendly way. Or it can operate by deep pressure, where what is effective is not the behaviour but the condemning attitude it expresses. It is not so much your tone of voice I mind, as the fact that you think worse of my character.

Yet being blamed by Schlick might not be like this. He treats blame as a form of punishment. He says, 'The question of who is responsible is the question concerning the *correct point of application of the motive* . . . It is a matter only of knowing who is to be punished or rewarded in order that punishment and reward function as such – be able to achieve their goal.'[7]

Suppose someone behaves badly to Schlick, maliciously spreading the false rumour that he has been converted to Hegelianism. Schlick, seeing him, may express his blame, speaking indignantly of his revulsion against this contemptible behaviour. But behind this speech may lie a cool calculation of how to influence the calumniator's motives. If the person being spoken to knows this, he may find it hard to accept in the way intended. Deep pressure may be more effective than surface pressure, but it may be self-defeating to adopt deep pressure as a conscious strategy.

There is a similar problem about our attitudes towards our own actions. Schlick says that to reproach myself for an act is to want myself to have different motives from those that caused it, and that 'to blame oneself means just to apply motives of improvement to oneself'. This may work if, like Schlick, we are satisfied with a soft determinist account of free action. But, if we accept the forger's reply, we may see the fact that we had undesirable motives as a piece of bad luck. Then, trying to change ourselves by blaming ourselves may fail. 'I shall apply motives of improvement to myself', I may say, but the required guilt feelings may not come flooding in.

This defence of our attitudes fails. We cannot switch on responses, whether to other people or to ourselves, simply because those responses would have good consequences. The responses depend on the belief that they have some other justification.

[7] Ibid., section 4.

A more sophisticated defence of these attitudes of blame recognizes that they are more than aspects of social control. P. F. Strawson defends them this way, arguing that, 'Our practices do not merely exploit our natures, they express them.'[8] On this view, blame and guilt are part of a whole range of responses involved in relationships, including gratitude, resentment, forgiveness, love, and hurt feelings. If determinism undermined praise and blame, it would undermine all these reactive attitudes, in favour of detached objectivity. But this objectivity does not seem a practical possibility. As Strawson says,

A sustained objectivity of inter-personal attitude, and the human isolation that would entail, does not seem to be something of which human beings would be capable, even if some general truth were a theoretical ground for it.[9]

And, Strawson argues, even if such sustained emotional detachment were possible, determinism would not leave it as the only rational option:

. . . we could choose rationally only in the light of an assessment of the gains and losses to human life, its enrichment or impoverishment; and the truth or falsity of a general thesis of determinism would not bear on the rationality of *this* choice.[10]

Strawson's attractive and subtle line of thought does more justice to these reactions than the simpler view of them as ways of manipulating people. But his defence of them makes some debatable assumptions.

First, he assumes that the reactive attitudes have to stand or fall together. ('Without the freedom to blame, no praise can gratify', as the motto of *Le Figaro* says.) But are these attitudes always so interdependent? Suppose we decide that love and gratitude enrich our lives, while blame and resentment make them poorer. How do we know that it is psychologically impossible to give up the second pair while keeping the first? To know this, we should need evidence from many failed attempts. It could be said that the impossibility is not psychological. You do not count as loving someone if you are not the slightest jealous if she goes off with someone else. There are some logical links of this kind. But many such links would have to

[8] P. F. Strawson: Freedom and Resentment, *Proceedings of the British Academy*, 1962.
[9] Ibid., page 197.
[10] Ibid., page 199.

be traced out in detail to show that the attitudes form an utterly indivisible system.

The other questionable assumption is that the issue is simply whether these attitudes make life better or worse. The hard determinist can accept that they make life better, but say regretfully that they have to be given up because they presuppose beliefs which determinism shows to be false or confused. He thinks they have an irrationality of a different kind from that considered by Strawson.

(Imagine a tribe whose lives are permeated by religion. They are worried by arguments for atheism, which seem to threaten their whole way of life. Then a philosopher from Vienna comes and tells them not to worry: religion can be defended as a useful way of getting people to do things. Some of the tribe, though not all, are reassured. Then a more subtle philosopher from Oxford visits them. He says their religion is interwoven with their whole life, and says they will be unable to give it up. He then says that, even if they could give up religion, atheism would not make this rational. The question of rationality is about whether religion enriches or impoverishes their lives. Most of them are quite reassured. But a few persisting doubters are left wondering whether an atheist can really pray.)

In the debate over whether free action is possible, both sides agree that in a determinist world (and perhaps in any world) the explanation of what we do, if traced back far enough, will lead to things outside our control. Any ideal of total self-creation is unattainable. There is an element of good or bad luck in what we are. In the related debate over the reactive attitudes, the hard determinist says that our attitudes presuppose the total self-creation that is unattainable. The soft determinist says that they presuppose less than this: perhaps just that people can influence their actions and characters in the way only a fatalist denies. This debate too seems to reach an impasse, as it is unclear how we can settle the issue of what our attitudes presuppose.

Because both versions of the debate end in what looks like a stalemate, hard determinism has not been defeated. So it is perhaps worth looking at the position of self-creation in a world where the hard determinist case is accepted.

What would the world of hard determinism be like?
====

A sophisticated hard determinist will accept some of the soft determinist case. Because accepting hard determinism involves no commitment to fatalism, it is not pointless to try to influence what I am like. My decisions can affect that, just as they can affect such things as whether there is an accident. So the threat posed by hard determinism to self-creation is not that attempting it is pointless.

The more serious threat is that to the reactive attitudes. Self-creation is bound up with such attitudes, both to ourselves and to other people. Yet it seems that, in a hard determinist world, these attitudes would either wither away, or linger on in a feeble form, like superstitions no one really believes in.

On this matter, the sophisticated hard determinist will again accept part of the soft determinist case. The soft determinist model of free action brings out real differences between cases of maximum possible freedom and other cases that fall short. The reactive attitudes are useful means of mutual influence, and are at the heart of our interwoven emotional lives. Sophisticated hard determinists can accept all this, but still say that the maximum possible freedom, because it retains an element of luck, is not enough to justify the reactive attitudes.

But it is wrong to say that the only responses to people in a hard determinist world will be coolly scientific. Reactions which presuppose desert will have to be given up. But a whole range of reactive attitudes are not desert-based. Consider the aesthetic-cum-sexual responses we have to people's appearance, or to their style and charm. We have aesthetic responses of another kind to people's intellectual qualities: to their being imaginative, independent, or quick on the uptake. These responses are not desert-based. We do not think people are attractive, or quick on the uptake, because of praiseworthy efforts they have made. On the contrary, these seem very clear cases of features owing a lot to luck. Perhaps this is one reason why we think of our responses to them as aesthetic rather than moral.

These responses will save the hard determinist from a totally dry emotional life. There seems no reason to stop at that point. There can also be aesthetic responses to people's motives and character. If I am a hard determinist, I can still admire someone's generosity, so long as I accept that this is in part good luck. It will be like admiring someone's musical talent. And, when someone swindles me, I can have similarly unfavourable responses to their character. My judgment that someone is repellently selfish in outlook will be like the judgment that someone has a repulsive smile.

These aesthetic responses could be conveyed to other people. And, just as people want to be thought physically attractive, rather than ugly, so people would care about aesthetic responses to their character. Desert-based attitudes, like blame, would have been renounced. But unfavourable aesthetic responses to character as revealed in actions might function like blame. They might be just as effective in putting pressure on people to change their behaviour.

And giving up pride, guilt, and other desert-based responses to our own actions would not eliminate all reactive attitudes to ourselves. Aesthetic responses parallel to the old desert-based ones could grow up. I could regret being selfish or dishonest in the way I regret having no talent for music or sport. I could judge my actions aesthetically as admirable or appalling, and these thoughts could be charged with feeling.

At this point there is a question. Are these emotionally charged aesthetic responses to my actions any different from pride or guilt? And do the aesthetic responses to other people's characters really differ from moral praise and blame? The boundary between hard and soft determinism starts to seem unclear. As hard determinism gets less schematic and crude, it incorporates responses which look less and less different from the desert-based attitudes it repudiates.

The result can be put in two ways. On one view, this is a triumph for hard determinism. We can expel desert-based attitudes and yet have emotions more warm-blooded than those appropriate to a psychiatrist or a social worker. On another view, this is the collapse of hard determinism. It accommodates responses only metaphysically distinguishable from those which by definition it repudiates.

We do not need to settle whether this upshot is a triumph for hard or for soft determinism. It is enough that it allows the kinds of reactive responses to ourselves which are needed for self-creation.

CHAPTER NINETEEN

WE

We owe a cornfield respect, not because of itself, but because it is food for mankind. In the same way, we owe our respect to a collectivity, of whatever kind – country, family or any other – not for itself, but because it is food for a certain number of human souls.

SIMONE WEIL: *The Need for Roots.*

A GROUP, WITH too many people for bonds of friendship, can have an identity of its own. Sometimes, as with a political or religious group, this identity is created by shared beliefs. But the larger groups that would probably most strike a Martian visitor are ethnic, linguistic and national groups, whose shared sense of identity is largely independent of shared beliefs.

The view from Mars

Go back to the Martian scientist, who looked at the way the personal frontier and the bodily frontier coincide. Suppose evolution has taken a very different course on Mars. There is still competition to survive, and, as here, genes for characteristics helping survival are favoured. But the characteristics with most survival value on Mars are different from those that flourish on Earth.

Creatures there are poisonous to each other if eaten, and the mutations that would allow carnivorous eating have not arisen. All Martians take their energy entirely from the sun. Cooperation against the Martian sandstorms is the most important characteristic for survival. Species with the most generous and intelligent forms of cooperation stand the best chance of surviving the storms. There have been no mutations to produce a strain of freeloaders who draw the benefits of cooperation without contributing.

The Martian who studied the evolution of life on Earth might be appalled by how different things are here. It might seem especially hellish that conscious creatures devour each other. The Martian might have the thought which the skeletons of carnivorous reptiles suggested to William James:

There is no tooth in any one of those museum-skulls that did not daily through long years of the foretime hold fast to the body struggling in despair of some fated living victim. Forms of horror just as dreadful to the victims, if on a small spatial scale, fill the world about us today. Here on our very hearths and in our gardens the infernal cat plays with the panting mouse, or holds the hot bird fluttering in her jaws. Crocodiles and rattlesnakes and pythons are at this moment vessels of life as real as we are; their loathsome existence fills every minute of every day . . .[1]

On Mars it is argued that a loving God could not have created the life found on Earth.

The Martian might be interested in the dominant species. Humans partly came to dominate in the appalling way characteristic of the planet: among their advantages, they were highly effective killers, intelligent enough to kill other species at a distance. And, in the early days of the species, the packs of human hunter-killers that survived were often those best at killing other packs of humans competing for the same places.

But, despite these origins of the species, the Martian might see some optimistic signs. Human consciousness developed at an extraordinary rate. Humans asked questions, and used their intelligence to start answering them. They had discovered how to make their knowledge grow, and used it to protect themselves against disease and other misery. They had love and friendship, and could be warm and generous. They delighted in their children. They developed play, a sense of humour, and an emotional response to the beauty of their world. They had fused the emotions and the imagination in creating poems, symphonies, religions, plays, paintings and novels. The species that emerged partly through being good at killing was inventing codes of ethics. It included pacifists and vegetarians.

Yet the Martian looking now would see the human species still deeply disfigured by its terrible origins. Many die of hunger, while many others care so little that they create mountains of unused food

[1] William James: *The Varieties of Religious Experience*, London, 1960, pages 169–170.

rather than send it to help. Humans can still be found to torture other humans with electric shocks or by tearing out their eyes. And they still live in tribes, with apparently unstoppable epidemics of mutual killing. This is now especially dangerous, as their methods of killing can destroy their whole species, together with most of the others on the planet. But many of them see this danger, and the species is groping for some new world order, for some way of living together peacefully. The question is whether this will come in time.

Some sources of group conflict

There is nothing at all in the Martian view to surprise us. (Like all 'Martian' thought experiments, it adopts what is really a particular human perspective.) This Martian view consists of familiar platitudes of the human condition. But, although we are deadened by their familiarity, the platitudes are true. The fact that they are so familiar makes them unstimulating topics for thought. And their importance makes it seem almost pretentious to discuss them. Yet reluctance to think about them may contribute to the solutions not coming in time.

Some of the roots of conflict must be in our psychology. Of course, to understand the causes of wars we need to know much that is not purely psychological. We need to understand the political and economic causes of arms races. We need the historian's perspective: how did nearly all of Europe manage to outgrow wars between Catholics and Protestants? What can anthropologists tell us about the differences between neighbouring communities that fight and those that live in peace? We need to know what the Theory of Games can tell us about mutual deterrence and about disarmament. I want to suggest some aspects of our psychology that may also be relevant. But this is not an alternative to answering the other questions. Psychological factors are not the only important ones.

When war is discussed in connection with human psychology, attention is usually directed on aggression. But this may be a distortion of emphasis.

We are familiar with aggression in everyday life. Two drivers, whose cars have collided, disagree about whose fault it was: tempers are lost, insults are exchanged and even a fight may start. *Perhaps* this is a model of what happens when countries go to war, or a political group starts a terrorist campaign. But we should not assume in advance that it is an adequate model. It may blind us to the role of cool calculation. And, even where decisions for war are accompanied by aggressive feelings, there may be longer-term psychological factors that are also important.

Some conflicts leading to mutual killing are ideological, or, in a broad sense, religious. What matters is that our system of belief should prevail. Central America must not go Communist. Central Europe must not go Capitalist. Catholic versus Protestant in Northern Ireland. Christianity versus Islam in the Lebanon. Our religion, or our political religion, should be defended or propagated, by force if necessary.

Other wars are at least partly tribal. Their tribe has insulted ours, or is occupying our land. 'Israel is ours' versus 'Palestine is ours'. 'The Falklands are British' versus 'The Malvinas are Argentinian'. Republicans versus Loyalists. (Some conflicts come in both lists.) Biafra versus Nigeria. Greek Cyprus versus Turkish Cyprus. Vietnamese versus Cambodians. Iran versus Iraq. These conflicts about whose flag should fly somewhere go on and on. No doubt there are other things which contribute to some of these conflicts, such as economic factors, or the need for land. But, when allowance has been made for these, there seems a stubborn residue of tribalism.

Perhaps, in understanding our conflicts, the psychology of Belief and of group loyalty is at least as important as that of aggression.

Tribalism and identity
==

The disastrous consequences of our tribalism are obvious. Why has it not withered away? Perhaps national or group identity is defended so strongly because of the part it plays in the sense people have of their individual identity.

Identification with a group needs a deeper explanation than the distinctive characteristics that members of the group have in common. Psychologists have found that when people are divided into two groups on the basis of trivial differences, or even when they know they have been allocated randomly, they develop a bias in favour of their own group. They discriminate in favour of members of their own group in sharing rewards, and evaluate fellow members more favourably. People develop stereotyped pictures of other groups, seeing individuals in terms of the stereotype. We look for and notice differences that reflect well on our group, and so boost our self-esteem. And there is some evidence that, when groups compete against each other, this improves the self-esteem of their members.[2]

Our interest in our own identity, and our partial creation of it, are central features of our psychology. Many of the things we most value are not the 'impersonal' pleasures that would be available to some isolated part of a fragmented brain. They transcend isolated experiences, and depend on our ability to make something coherent of ourselves and what we do. This is why the version of utilitarianism that values only pleasure is implausible. Imagine a life like that of H. M.: what you do fades out of your memory a few moments later. You have no inner story about yourself, and cannot carry out any sustained projects, whether of self-creation or anything else. Some might choose such a life, if it included permanent intense pleasure. But others (most of us, I believe) would not. We would care less about pleasure than about being denied relationships, the chance of achieving things, and the chance of making something of our lives and ourselves.

The values which make us see the blissful oblivion as so meaningless also play a disturbing part in the psychology of our conflicts. Our tribalism, and our loyalty to political and other religions, are bound up with emotions that go very deep. Their hold on us depends on the way these loyalties contribute to our sense of ourselves.

I have two worries about this claim. One is lack of proof. It is a plausible claim, but I have no way of refuting a persistent sceptic. As often with the more interesting parts of psychology, decisive evidence is hard to come upon. At least, I have not come upon it. The claim can be taken as a conjecture, as an invitation to try to refute it. The other worry is the opposite. Perhaps it is so obviously true that it is just a platitude. To me it sometimes does seem to have this degree of obviousness. But I have not seen it made explicit, and perhaps making it so will expose otherwise unnoticed weaknesses. (I hope it escapes the fate of being both a boring platitude *and* false.)

Just as a species may flourish in a particular ecological niche, so the development of individual personality may depend on the support of a group. Like climbing plants searching for something to hook on to, we look for such support even where, as with the random allocation

---

[2] John C. Turner: Social Identification and Psychological Group Formation, in H. Tajfel (ed.): *The Social Dimension*, Cambridge, 1984, volume 2.

of the psychology experiments, the group has no shared basis. But, as climbing plants flourish where there is support, so our sense of ourselves flourishes in groups with enough in common to take on a life of their own.

This dependence on the shared understanding of a group is brought out by differences of language. When you speak a foreign language poorly, you have to say simpler things than you would like. In doing so, you present a simplified version of yourself. (This does not only apply to talking another language. It can also hold in another country where they speak a version of your own language. Turns of phrase, humour, and tones of voice are part of a 'language' which may be different. One way of drawing the boundaries of a culture is to take the region where such signals are understood.)

These communities of shared meanings draw on shared experiences. (Think of the private languages and jokes in families, drawing on common experience of monstrously pretentious neighbours or holiday luggage disasters.) The experiences shared by a community are preserved in its history. It it because of the part played by this shared past in the sense of the group's identity that people care so much about history being tampered with.

Some of the attempts made to rewrite history are grotesque. Milan Kundera describes a photograph of Gottwald in 1948, addressing a crowd from a Prague balcony, flanked by other party leaders. One of them, Clementis, gave his fur cap to protect Gottwald's head from the snow. The photograph was reproduced everywhere and became known to everyone. Later, Clementis was hanged. He was removed from Czech history, and from the photograph. 'All that remains of Clementis is the cap on Gottwald's head.'[3]

This kind of behaviour is comic, but also sad and threatening. People hope to be remembered: it is sad to think of every trace of someone being obliterated. But the obliteration also threatens the shared memory and understanding that creates the identity of a community. To know that your children are being systematically lied to about events you experienced or played a part in must sometimes create despair. (Imagine what would happen to the shared meanings of a family if false information was systematically fed to them about each other's pasts: 'Your father has many convictions for

[3] Milan Kundera: *The Book of Laughter and Forgetting*, translated by Michael Henry Heim, London, 1982.

sexual assault on children, but he is a pathological liar and will do anything to conceal his past from you.')

The persistence of our tribalism is partly explained by the way individuality flourishes inside the shared understanding of a group. People resist threats to the identity of their group, in the way a coastal community resists threats to its fishing grounds.

Groups and recognition

The nation state is one of the clearest expressions of group identity. The frontiers of the nation state do not always coincide with the boundaries of shared identity. Linguistic, racial or religious divisions can be deeper. But, when these other groupings are seen as more important, there is often some aspiration towards separate nationhood. Why is the shared identity of a group so often expressed as nationalism?

Defence of a shared language and culture is only part of an explanation. For many cases of rivalry with another group, or even of being dominated by one, do not involve a real threat to cultural survival. The motive can be the need for recognition. Just as we care about the individual recognition that a group context can provide, so we care that the recognition is not devalued by the group being slighted.

It is sometimes argued that Black Africans have a higher standard of living in South Africa than they would in any other African country. This of course does not answer the obvious criticisms of the inequalities within the country. But, even more, this kind of argument ignores the non-economic needs of people. How could there not be a nationalist movement where, on the basis of race, the majority in a country are deprived of political power, and humiliated by being treated as inferior beings?

(Non-economic motives for nationalism are not confined to Black South Africans. The brother of the former Prime Minister John Vorster described his schooling at the time of the First World War: 'If you were caught speaking Afrikaans, you had to carry a placard round your neck bearing the words "I must not speak Dutch." When the bell went for school to start again the last man with what was called the Dutch mark, had to write out one thousand times "I must speak English at school."'[4] It is not hard to guess the con-

[4] Quoted in David Harrison: *The White Tribe of Africa*, Johannesburg, 1981, page 54.

tribution this kind of thing made to the Afrikaner nationalism whose effects Black Africans now feel.)

It is sometimes said that members of the Catholic community in Northern Ireland have a higher standard of living than they would in the Republic. But a Nationalist might deny that this is adequate compensation for the slights Catholics receive in being treated as second-class citizens. Something similar applies to members of the Protestant community. It could be argued that it would pay them to buy off the violence by agreeing to join the Republic. But a Unionist might reply that his community would then lose political control over their lives, and suffer a loss of recognition and respect.

The Northern Irish case brings out the way in which threats to cultural survival are not the whole story. No language is threatened. And if the Republic were to declare cultural pluralism, with Protestants allowed their own history books, as well as abortion and contraception, it is hard to see this making much dent in Unionism. Parallel things could be said about how Nationalism would survive similar concessions within Northern Ireland to the Catholic community. The removal of threats of cultural erosion might not remove the anxieties of either group about recognition and respect. Often, nothing short of self-governing nationhood seems enough to do that. And this is a problem where, as with Northern Ireland, or with Israelis and Palestinians, two groups claim the same place.

Perhaps one small piece of progress would be to see the problems clearly and to recognize their size. If the suggestion here is correct, group loyalties are bound up with individuals' sense of their own identity. The connections can be simply stated. Concern with identity creates a need for recognition. And we want that recognition to be validated: the group that gives it must in turn be given similar recognition and respect. Any successful erosion of tribalism will have to take account of these very deep roots in our psychology.

Our disastrous tribal and religious loyalties are so deeply rooted because they grow out of things we would not give up. The attitudes leading to barbarity and killing are not a chance addition to human nature, but are perversions of some of our deepest values. Our dilemma is that the most destructive and dangerous part of our nature is tied so closely to much of what gives point to our lives.

If this picture is right, there is the question: can our awareness of these connections help us weaken these loyalties or help reduce their harmfulness?

There seem two possibilities worth considering. One is that we might weaken the loyalties by moving towards a world where the same needs can partly be met in different ways. The other is that, even if these loyalties are unlikely to fade away, our greater self-awareness about them may cause them to take a less harmful form.

Alternatives

Tribalism and Belief contribute to our sense of our identity. But obviously they do not make the only contribution. People do not have to think of themselves primarily in terms of being Black or White, French, Russian, Jewish, British or Afrikaner. Nor need they build their identity mainly around being Catholic or Islamic, Marxist or Conservative. There are alternatives based on relationships and on personal style, or on self-expression through work and other activity. Those who find fulfilment as parents or friends, as doctors, comedians, chefs, sculptors or teachers, may not see being White or being Protestant as a very important part of their lives. Recognition is still a need, but this can come from groups unlikely to be warlike: the patients I cure, or those who eat at the restaurant where I am chef.

The hope of reducing the need for tribalism and Belief is a reason for favouring a society in which things are arranged to provide the maximum opportunity for self-expression and for mutual recognition. Of course this hope is not the only reason for wanting such a society: self-creation and self-expression matter for their own sake. But it adds to the case for a society where people have a lot of freedom to direct their lives. It adds to the case for a society with more opportunity of satisfying work, and so where less of people's potential goes to waste.

It is fortunate that the things which might weaken the need for tribalism are, independently, features of a good society. It is unfortunate that bringing them about, while a daunting task, is such an uncertain cure for tribalism.

In Britain, support for the National Front does not seem exceptionally strong among those recognized for their creativity or achievements. But we need evidence from different cultures: are racism and fascism in Western European countries more common among those either unemployed or in dreary jobs? And what about other forms of tribalism? Who are the people most and least free from tribalism in Northern Ireland? Are the answers the same in Cyprus, and in Lebanon? Have Jews who have been most creative and fulfilled been less interested than others in their Jewish identity? Has nationalism faded in societies with great personal freedom?

I do not know the answers to these questions. And, without answers to them, it is impossible to be confident that a society shaped to allow greater opportunities for self-expression and recognition would weaken tribalism. It is a plausible hypothesis, but not more than that. Yet, since it suggests creating a society that is desirable on other grounds, we should perhaps act on the hypothesis, unproved as it is. We lose nothing by putting it to the test

Growing up
==

The tribalism and Belief that create our conflicts will not be eliminated easily or soon. Perhaps they meet other needs, as well as those concerned with identity. And perhaps their contribution to the sense of identity will not easily be replaced. So, as well as looking for alternatives to tribalism and Belief, we need to consider if there are ways in which they can flourish harmlessly. (The rider sometimes has to steer the horse where it wants to go.)

We could consider oblique strategies of control. Just as we try to avoid things that make us angry or depressed, so we may come to avoid things that trigger our emotional dogmatism or our tribalism. And, where the tribalism and Belief are not ours, we may become more sensitive to the need not to trample on things that are food for a certain number of human souls.

But, more fundamentally, our self-awareness may in itself help to change this part of our psychology. Through becoming self-conscious about the deep roots of tribalism and Belief, as well as about their dangers, we may change their nature.

We have seen how awareness of the vulnerability of beliefs, both to evidence and to revisions in other parts of our system, makes us *unable* to be simple Believers any more. Something similar may be true of awareness of the sources of tribalism. Perhaps simple-minded nationalism and patriotism will become impossible for us. A more sophisticated tribalism might be one where the tribe gives us recognition and a sense of belonging, but where we no longer take it at face value, or so seriously. (It is one sign of a civilized country if the national anthem is heard with a mixture of mild embarrassment and jokiness, rather than with emotion-choking seriousness.)

It may seem that the growth of self-awareness is an impossibly slow way of eroding tribalism, and gives no hope of our conflicts fading before they destroy us. To trust it may seem a regression to nineteenth-century illusions of steady and reliable progress towards a more civilized condition. Among the twentieth-century lessons we have all learnt are that such progress is not inevitable, and that the darker side of human nature has not disappeared.

The point about the slowness of changes in human consciousness is a real one. But the suggestion is not that these changes should be our only strategy against conflict. Obviously we need political agreements, ways of containing the arms race, arbitration procedures, and so on. Perhaps more than anything, we need to select national leaders who are not fanatical or hysterical. But these short-term devices need to be supplemented by slower and deeper changes in consciousness if we are to survive in the long run. They are not alternatives.

The other point, about our loss of nineteenth-century optimism, is also a real one. We all know the great monuments to human barbarism erected since then, and the news every day gives smaller reminders of the darker side of our nature. But we may have reacted too far, and may underrate the growth of human consciousness.

Our view of human nature is more like the Martian view than it is like the nineteenth-century one. The things that have shocked us result from combining barbarism with modern technology. When barbarism is so much more effective, it stops looking like a minor part of us that is fading away. But the Martian view had a longer perspective, looking back to our evolutionary origins. We emerged as packs of hunters and killers, and our whole history has been disfigured by tribal wars and by revolting cruelty. Perhaps what is new, in this longer perspective, is the slow and faltering attempt since the eighteenth century to move away from this. Because of the visible horrors, we may underrate how far we have come.

We are subject to three kinds of illusion here. The long, slow growth of human consciousness is almost imperceptible. But it does take place. Through science, we understand the world better, and there has been a growth of scepticism about varieties of Belief unsupported by evidence. We see mental illness as needing help rather than ridicule. In many parts of the world, we do not crucify people, or disembowel them; we do not kill or mutilate law-breakers. Many societies do not let their members starve, and it is coming to seem unacceptable that people anywhere should starve. Day by day, these long, slow changes in the climate of opinion cannot be detected. Children do not change on a daily basis either, but they do grow up.

The second illusion is the 'materialist' belief that changes in the climate of opinion do not matter. Political and economic changes are much more visible, and their importance is obvious. But to write off the more intangible changes would be to assume that the prevailing climate of thought makes no important difference to what life is like: that we are only seriously different from medieval people in economics and technology.

The third illusion is that changes in the climate of opinion are so large and slow that what we do as individuals makes no difference to them. This is to confuse making an imperceptible contribution with making no contribution. There is a great difference between many people making an imperceptible contribution and the same people each making no contribution. There is a difference between a town where everyone puts their ice cream wrapper in the bin and one where each person drops it in the street, saying, 'Mine won't make any difference.' We wrongly suppose that what we do and say makes no difference to the growth of human consciousness, because we overlook the cumulative effects of individual contributions each below the threshold of visibility. The movement of consciousness away from tribalism and Belief could involve the kind of collective decision that is made up of millions of little decisions. Since the eighteenth century, the decent hope of more thoughtful people has been that tribal and religious loyalties may come to take second place to a more general humanism. Since 1914, and even more since 1945, we have started to see the urgency of this process of growing up. But any day's news is a reminder of how far we have to go. Perhaps, seeing why these loyalties have such a hold on us will help us. If we understand tribalism and Belief better, we may find less destructive ways of meeting the needs they satisfy. Perhaps, in a suitably cautious and uncoercive way, we – the human race – may try a little collective self-creation.

INDEX